NICK OF TIME

NICK OF TIME

Women Write About Art and Aging

JULIE LANDSMAN, DEBRA J STONE,
AND MORGAN GRAYCE WILLOW
Editors

MINNESOTA

University of Minnesota Press
Minneapolis
London

Published by the University of Minnesota Press
111 Third Avenue South, Suite 290
Minneapolis, MN 55401-2520
http://www.upress.umn.edu

ISBN 978-1-5179-2045-6 (pb)

A Cataloging-in-Publication record for this book is available from the Library of Congress.

Printed in the United States of America on acid-free paper

35 34 33 32 31 30 29 28 27 26 10 9 8 7 6 5 4 3 2 1

Contents

Introduction

Tell Me Your Diamonds

JULIE LANDSMAN, DEBRA J STONE,
AND MORGAN GRAYCE WILLOW

A gathering of color, of song, of dance, of words, poems, and stories created by painters, singers, dancers, and writers makes up this collection. Each woman reflects on how aging has changed or affected her art. Some of us grew up on rock and roll, others on Leonard Bernstein or on rap and hip-hop. The years, as they accumulate, touch us in varied ways, bringing grief, joy, anger, laughter, tears, exhaustion. Yet each of us has found a way to create work out of language, in song, on canvas, or on fine watercolor paper. We've worked in studios, at kitchen and dining room tables, out in the hills of Italy, and on plane trips. We envisioned a collection of stories and thoughts that captures the challenges and accomplishments of elder women artists growing older in a youth culture. In our call for women creatives over sixty-three years of age, we received submissions from established and emerging artists in Minnesota.

The Introduction's title comes from Toni Morrison's novel *Beloved.* The character Beloved has a hunger for Sethe's stories, and by asking for "diamonds," Beloved is asking her mother to share details of her life. These requests give Sethe a sense of fulfillment as she begins to share her stories, and we, too, have asked our contributors of elder women artists to tell their stories, their diamonds.

We write here in essay, mixed genre, in poetry, in long sentences. Twenty-seven women, ages sixty-five to ninety-three, create worlds: paint and draw, write and tango, walk to the river, ride bikes along lake paths, attend conferences or retreats, stay at home. Some of us arrived from refugee camps; others grew up on farms or in suburbs.

Minnesota is unique in what it gives us: spaces to engage with our art and our writing with others, be it a class or writing studio at the Loft Literary Center or Minnesota Center for Book Arts. In summer and in the chill of a Minnesota winter, many of us join our neighbors to create a poster for a street festival, a rehearsal for a summer park performance, a celebration of Indigenous people. We bring cultural variety with us: Latina, European American, Asian, African American, African, Middle Eastern, Hmong, and many more communities arrive each year.

There is history here of women and their advocacy for the arts: the Women's Art Registry of Minnesota and WARM Gallery, both founded and run by women. SASE: The Write Place, More Than a Single Story, Mizna—these are just some of the unique groups that have sprung up in neighborhoods and towns to go alongside the Minnesota State Arts Board grants for writers and artists. Even more specifically, women have led classes in poetry for those in memory care, summer programs for kids engaging in the arts, and more rigorous engagement for access and fairness for women. In this way, we encourage all children, especially girls, to dream big and to see around them a future in creativity and community.

In Minnesota, we are surrounded by elders who may have been born in another country and who bring their own passion with them. We are surrounded by so many vibrant new arrivals that our work, our communities, change and adapt and are richer for it. You will come to know in this collection a remarkable variety of art by elder women who still advocate for our place in this world, reaching many with dance, words, paintings, song.

A variety of form and genre enlivens this volume. From classic essay, monologue, historical reflection, poetry, letters home, and memoir, this book encompasses a rich array of unique voices describing each woman's connection to her world. Each woman observes in her own way the passage of time, her life as an artist, and how the two intersect. Each woman in this book has put into words what they do, the sources they draw from, and how aging affects their artistic life. Or, by contrast, finds that aging hasn't made a great difference in their work. What is so powerful in this collection is honesty in each piece. There is a clarity in each woman's unflinching desire to continue working through the changes that come with time. In our own voices, visions, poems, portraits, landscapes, or shape-shifting abstractions, we find what moves us and, perhaps, also moves you, Dear Reader.

Our hope is that you find a chord here, one that strikes from a place of appreciation for the infinite variety in elder women's lives. You might be enriched in your own experience of aging or in how you view elders around you. As women we bring similarity as well as difference one from another. We believe we can see how fortunate we are, even in the midst of sexism, racism, antigay voices, and the stereotypes of aging, to span this experience of years. Getting to know the women in this anthology leaves us, the editors, with a deepened respect for our differences as well as our similarities. And finally, a salute to the humor that accompanies us as we age. It's not always doom and gloom but often joy and laughter at our eccentric ways in this world.

We do well to note Hazel Belvo, well-known painter, professor, and arts advocate, who wrote: "Something an important artist said to me when I was young and I never forgot it: 'people don't know or acknowledge that artists are people too.' Much of what I read in history that is meaningful to me is about artists' lives and relationships and what makes them human. Just think about Virginia Woolf and her sister, the painter Vanessa Bell, and the writings about them, about Gertrude Stein and Alice B. Toklas. About all of us, who continue to make a place in our busy lives for our art." For the title of this collection, we were inspired by Bonnie Raitt's song "Nick of Time" about a resurgence of love late in life. Just as "Life gets mighty precious" during the last stretch of time available to us, love, in its many forms, can heal and rejuvenate. Among forms of love is creativity: our own ability to generate new work despite—perhaps also because of—the awareness of limitation. The women in this anthology have committed themselves to continuing their lifelong journey through this final "nick" of time.

Acknowledgments

We could not have brought this book to fruition without the community that has surrounded us each step of the way. It is a testament to the creative women and men in various places at various stages of our endeavor that made *Nick of Time* possible. We want to thank Sun Yung Shin, who guided and advised us in the early stages of this project and helped us shape the concept. We are deeply grateful to Carolyn Holbrook, whose enthusiasm and active support of this project from early on opened doors for us. She is instrumental in helping put this volume in your hands. We thank Rebecca Pavlenko, who opened her beautiful photography studio to us for a gathering of contributors for sharing thoughts and experiences about being an elder woman in the arts. Our heartfelt thanks go to Erik Anderson, our editor at the University of Minnesota Press, who enthusiastically embraced this project and guided us with humor and insight all along the way. To Emma Saks and the entire team at the University of Minnesota Press, our thanks for their support and skill in bringing the book into physical being. To our contributors, thank you. There would be no anthology without your words. We are also grateful to each other for the gift of collaboration. It's been such pleasure to puzzle out how to bring this anthology to life together.

Aging While Making Art

HEND AL-MONSOUR

As I aged, I got to know me better. I gained some wisdom and insight but lost some sharpness and agility. I will share with you an insight and a challenge.

The Insight

My inner observer stayed ageless as I expanded in some abilities and diminished in others. She peeks from her secure niche with a nonjudgmental sense of self. In a sense, she is judgmental, but her judgment focuses on others. Sometimes, she tells me, "Look at that old woman. She is sixty and wants to learn belly dancing." When I tell her I am sixty-seven and want to learn animation, she shrugs dismissively; she thinks she is above aging.

This ageless *I* is one of many. They constellated over the years and came into focus slowly as a pantheon of deities; each has her realm, attributes, and way of reining me in. If I ponder, I can discover the peculiar characteristics of each deity and when they like to visit and take control. I can glimpse how those different *I*'s interact, coexist, and give space to each other. For example, they all disappear when I am about to give a public speech, except for the self-doubting *I*, which then dominates.

I often find myself in an imaginary heated conversation with an opponent to my argument. I give this opponent the persona of someone outside of me, but in reality, this persona is one of my *I*'s.

I learned that my motivations for making art are not what I consciously say they are. The conscious *I* gives a logical statement for the artwork, but that is not the whole truth. The real meaning of the piece, what it truly communicates, is too deep for this conscious *I* to grasp. I realize now that making art is like dreaming. You can recount the dream in tedious details but don't know what it means. Yet, it had communicated what it wanted. Dreams give us the feedback, processing, and deep cleansing our *I*'s need.

Similarly, whether we make it or view it, artwork communicates with us on a deeper level—more profoundly than we know consciously. Art connects individuals and communities through generations and across geography through invisible threads. Those threads make us humans. Years ago, after I gave a passionate presentation of one of my pieces and how it meant to protest discrimination against women in a religious text, my art mentor at the time said, "But it is beautiful!" I realized then that the piece was rather celebratory. The text and images were composed harmoniously with vibrant colors. That was one of my early glimpses of the *I*'s under my skin. The infuriated rebellious *I* went through the holy book and picked up every diminishing word related to women, while the tradition-loving *I* depicted it lovingly. After that critique, I learned to indulge both *I*'s, the one who challenges and the one who admires my cultural practices.

The Challenge

Upon coming to America, I discovered that adults could attend school and get more education. What a fantastic concept! I had gotten burned out as a doctor and wanted to pursue my artistic career. I was in my forties; aging was not an issue because I looked youthful. I went back to school and studied art, which was a blast. Since then,

I am still learning because I love it. I am always learning or wanting to learn something. I subscribe to several online learning platforms, receive continuing education newsletters from several schools, and am forever taking a class. Perhaps this is a complex, but I enjoyed it and did not think anything of it until I got gray-haired. On the one hand, yes, I am not the fast learner I once was, but on the other, I am still thirsty to know more. I can learn and comprehend new knowledge more deeply than when I was young.

Being old is not a hindrance to learning. *Looking old* is. In neutral states, the ageless *I* is happily oblivious that I look old. But looking old is reflected in the eyes of Uber drivers, waitpersons, cashiers, and any new acquaintance. I say I have a class. They look at my gray hair and ask me where I teach. Do they think they will offend me if they think I am a student? Or does it even cross their minds?

I feel wary when I am the oldest person in the class, including the teacher. Everybody is too respectful toward me. Perhaps I look wise and mature. My ripe facade intimidates people and hinders my learning. My learner *I* is frustrated. I want to continue learning, but I am increasingly finding myself out of place. In my Arabic upbringing, older adults should leave the stage for the young. "One should not take her time plus another's time" is an Arabic proverb that means you have only one shot at anything and can do it only at the proper time. I think that is what my ageless *I* internalized. It's time to reeducate her.

But is it true? Does learning while old mean taking someone else's chances? Or do mature people have the same right to education? What about young people with bright minds but no education opportunities?

Now, the *egalitarian I* is talking. And so on.

I Ain't Your Side Chick and Other Things You Need to Know About This Old Woman

AMOKE KUBAT

I don't have a problem with getting old. I knew it was going to happen. As a former Trekkie, I believe in other worlds. I remain sci-fi curious and adventurous. Getting old is a new frontier. Maybe. I do believe that death is not the final destination. Time is no longer my adversary. Time is wealth: an energetic currency for mind, body, emotion, and spiritual connectivity and interactions. No nickel and diming for me. I HOLLA for my DOLLA!

I'm using my time to become a transformative human being, living beyond the limitations of the mind and body: what has never been understood, seen, or imagined. Some days my feet walk a steady path. Other days I fall or fail in this aspiration, but I keep getting up. However, I do have a huge problem with how others burden me with their disdain and fears about getting old. Getting old is not becoming nonhuman. Or less productive. Or disabled. At seventy-three, I am succulent. I'm not dried up or mentally withered. My memories are rich and detailed.

I really never gave much attention to getting old. I've always been aware that I live in a world dominated by other people's cultural angst about aging. In my eyes aging didn't register as an issue. I watched for my own crow's-feet. I wanted those Maasai-like neck ring grooves around my throat: the best place for a string of pearls. I wanted my grandmother's soft pillowy lap that rested a child's head perfectly. I rejoiced at forty-three, at the first strands of gray!

Give *me* that silver-tipped cane that went with those church white gloves and spotless orthopedic shoes. I want that Old Woman Swagger, imbued with spiritual authority, as I navigate my life on this swiftly tilting planet. Older Black women possess these magnificent attributes. In my younger mind, these were Purple Heart medals for surviving and thriving. Having wisdom. Caretaking and serving. Becoming an Elder. Walking one's road with dignity to fulfill one's destiny and, most important, the keys to entering the Realm of Ancestors.

I grew up eavesdropping on old womenfolk. I learned to be the fly on the wall. I leaned into their whispered conversations. The juiciest intel was spoken in snippets of Pig Latin. They shared insights into their internal worlds. They spoke candidly about dreams and hopes. They shared their Black women's fragilities and perceived failures as they did each other's hair, shared their best dishes, or played cards. I enjoyed their private Testifying and Shit Talking that often broke loose while sipping a *lil' somethin' somethin'*. Usually a sherry. Mogen David wine. Something stronger, distilled, on the rocks for those delicate topics, disappointments, and their shames: having a "slow child" that could never leave the house, domestic abuse, a run-around husband, a son on dope, a daughter's bastard, or maybe that menopausal pregnancy of their own.

But often, I heard the celebratory grandstanding and the complimentary declaration: BLACK DON'T CRACK. They lavished praises on those with flawless smooth skin and full heads of long, thick hair. Black skin held magical secrets for warding off the inevitable, getting old, a bit longer. Longevity, highly esteemed, was the goal, not remaining childish or youthful.

Old Black women always kept it real. Life wears a body out. It didn't matter if you lived your life large or small. Body parts simply wore out. Nobody expected one pair of shoes to last a lifetime. Your body was like a favorite dress. In time, it became too big, too small, faded, threadbare, or just unfashionable. But not disposable. Old Black women were always creatives. Old dresses transformed into new clothes for some fast-growing child, became kitchen curtains that flapped in soft summer breezes, or a heavy winter quilt that kept six kids in a bed warm.

Getting old comes with pain. Old Arthur (osteoarthritis) is a real formidable foe. He mounts and relentlessly rides a body that lived a laborious life. Old women rubbed gnarled knuckles and twisted knees. They rocked, stretching kinks from bowed spines and knotted muscles. A hot flash could randomly turn an unsuspecting woman into a stripper or a serial killer. Liniment, rubbing alcohol, Lydia E. Pinkham, hot water bottles, unlabeled suppositories, and home brews were stored arsenals. Getting old, death, and the devil were interchangeable forces. I understood death as a promise. Expiration date is unknowable but definitely coming for me. I don't dwell on it.

Maybe somewhere in a corner of my mind was a smidgin of antiaging awareness. I brushed my hair to encourage thickness and length. I scrubbed my teeth for whiteness and to keep all thirty-two. I kept my pleasantly plump body clean and greased. I grew up with one serious admonishment and practice: NO ASHY SKIN! Being ashy was you looking whitish or gray. Dead. An ashy child was perceived as not being loved or cared for. For an adult, it was the public reveal of a lack of concern and care for one's body. Grown-ups slathered me in Jergens lotion, petroleum jelly, Dixie Peach, cocoa butter, Crisco (in an emergency), and, in desperation, spit, to prevent any "ashiness" on my dirt-brown skin. Today I love jojoba and coconut oils.

Grown-ups pushed me to drink water. Water was the liquid cure for whatever torments a body. Head hurts. Drink water. Stomach queasy. Drink water. Cramps. Drink water. Bored. Drink water? I always hated the taste of water. Water tasted "tinny," like food from a can. Water only tasted good when cold or from a garden hose. I have few regrets, but I wish I had drunk more water. Water prevents the onset of many chronic illnesses that plague Black women's bodies: diabetes, high blood pressure, fibroids, and obesity. Being hydrated the blood flows throughout the body better. Lubricated joints keep you upright and mobile. Water helps the body easily eliminate potential dis-eases. Hindsight may be the best thing about getting old. Drinking more water is a priority.

I'm growing awareness, curiosity, and sometimes dismay about my aging process. People, places, and things are shape-shifting. When a beloved or popular celebrity's passing is revealed, I feel the approach of my own mortality. It took decades for me to find resignation for John Lennon's death. We shared mother wounds. The opening line for one of his songs, "Mother you had me but I never had you," felt like a shared longing or secret. I still mourn Prince.

Despite being called an Elder, I'm sought for solving perplexing Other People's Problems; lending-my-voice invites to parties are few. When invited, I cannot attend. Younger able-bodied people don't think about safety as I must. They're not thinking about the necessity for secure handrails, steps, stairs, elevators, locations of bathrooms, handicapped seating and parking, well-lit streets, and having an escort for my departures to my car. It is exhausting having to second-guess my daily routines. Trip, slip, and fall factors lurk as an underfoot cat, spilled liquids, small rocks and twigs. I frequently take Metro Mobility, the adult shorty bus. It is *not* a luxury car or even reliable. Lyft and Uber drivers are not always safe or helpful. I've been left curbside on a one-hundred-degree day to find my way to an unmarked address.

I've grown weary educating those who seem to know everything but lack the ability to respond to basic human needs. My needs. Many jump to help me, extending what they think I need, never asking or dismissing what I tell them. Falling in public is humiliating. I damn near need a tow truck to get upright again. It is disappointing that some of these are well-intentioned friends and organizations. I accept a few invitations now. I also say no a lot. I give no explanations. No is a complete sentence. I am not a side chick that is called 24/7 to relieve others' perturbations, loneliness, or pain. I'm not the trash can or toilet for your sadness, rage, angst dumping. I am not your free service for your pitiful and self-absorbed "self-care and reflection." All this handicaps me from my quality of life, my peace of mind. Find and pay for a caring, compassionate counselor. Not a therapist. Funny words: The. Rapist. I need to keep enough caring and compassion for myself. With too much going on, it is easy to fall into a pit of despair and drown. It does not mean I love anybody less. It means that I have learned to love my Black womanist self more.

Seriously, I recognize my telltale changes of aging. What I could do yesterday is not promised to be done today. I wake up grateful and praising spirit for the new day. I no longer spring out of bed and hit the ground running. My body snaps, crackles, and pops more and more. I open the oven to look for eggs. I know I am forgetful. I write lists for things I need to do. Words don't find my mouth and tongue. I stop mid-sentence or repeat myself. I have told others that I am "googling." The discomfort I see in their faces hurts me. Patience is now a superpower.

Memories of people, places, and things have become elusive. I have only a handful of combined family and friends who share and hold my herstory. They are the verifiers of the whos, whats, and what-the-hells of my random thoughts. Or dreams? When you get old, you don't sleep much at night.

Some days, my body betrays my mind. My mind betrays my heart. My heart fights to remain open and begs my spirit to stay as I work things out. The Old Black Woman Swagger eludes me. Without my cane or walker, I move like a toddler. My body does a gangster sideways roll. Early mornings or bad weather days, I move like Frankenstein's monster, my arms out, stepping heavily as I attempt to get to the bathroom. I'm amazed at the melodious musicality of my sphincter. I have been a whole orchestra! I often laugh at myself.

I'm making peace with my changing body. I have a beard. I shave. These chin hairs are diverse: one singular silver one and a patch of short, dark, curly ones. My waist-length locs are gone. My crown is thinning. Down below is bald. I'll not be needing a Brazilian bikini wax in my remaining lifetime.

My biggest hang-up about getting old is the possibility of never having another lover. It's not that I think I don't deserve love. I feel some kind of way of bringing all my life's baggage (and now health issues) into a new relationship. I always wanted to grow old with somebody. I wanted a long slow dance with the soundscapes of Motown music. I wanted a wildflower approach to friendship and intimacy. I wanted a partnership where we both tilled the soil, planted seeds, watered, weeded, and smelled the harvests of our highest intent for being loving human beings. I wanted to walk a shared memory lane of the good, bad, and ugly.

In all honesty, sometimes, I do mourn the bloom of youth. Old people are like babies. Babies are fearless! There are countless books on how to raise them. Getting older doesn't come with books on how to grow and be. There are few conversations to guide us through the next leg of our journey. Who do you ask about getting old? Adult diapers? Sexual health? I am more frightened about "coming and going" than losing my mind.

I admit that I'm scared death will take more loved ones. I don't want to lose any more. I can count my family on both hands now. Many of my friends died in their fifties or sixties. Those living have succumbed to debilitating physical and mental illnesses. I fear losing my eyesight or hearing. I can't imagine not being able to read or listen to music. I fear becoming isolated in my home due to losing my ability to leave it. I feel pure terror to even think I could be displaced from my home: in residential care, needing palliative or hospice services. Elder abuse is real.

I'm driven by the notion that my house must be clean and tidy the day I die! It's not about other people's judgment. I've always possessed an impressive amount of *I don't give a fuckism.* Maybe a coping strategy, but it worked for me. It grew from a life of hardships after my mother's early death. A clean house is my statement that, to the very end, I had as much control of my life as a Black woman in this anti-Black, misogynistic, ableist, and ageist society could.

Aging and my artistry emerged almost simultaneously. After retirement, I have been teaching for twenty-five years. I wasn't sure I was an artist. I hadn't produced anything artsy. A fifteen-year work in progress story, about Black mothers, became my self-published memoir, *Missing Mama: My Story of Loss, Sorrow and Healing,* in 2012.

I've written plays: *ANGRY BLACK WOMAN & Well Intentioned White Girl* (2016), *Old Good Pussy and Good Old Pussy* (2020), and *Opera of Memories* (2022). These works involved significant artistic learning curves. They were also markers to my realization about my capacities and abilities. Two scenes were cut from my performance of *Old Good Pussy.* One reason was due to time. The second was because I wasn't able to get into a costume, in the dark, in thirty seconds, without the use of both hands. I needed my cane or walker. The audience didn't miss these deleted acts. My performance was well received. However, I became depressed. I so wanted to dance in a winged costume that sparkled with white and colorful lights. I was crushed that I couldn't do something so simple. I felt the doors to my future closing. My third play, my most personal, was *Opera of Memories.* It's about an Old Woman who revisits her life as she takes objects from a box. The theater was very supportive of my needs. They built a handrail for me to access the stage (and post-play they added a small electric lift). I had two mature mentors who understood aging and disabilities. The Spirit of Memory was my personal assistant. I'm proud of this work. I know it was possibly my last public performance. I'm okay with this.

Now, simple household chores are time consuming and often painful in getting them done. Sometimes my body just can't keep up. Bending, stretching, standing, and toting are no longer absolutes. I've never been good at asking for help. I learned a long time ago who, how, and when you ask for help. I used my eyes and ears but not common sense. I got burned many times. I learned to trust my intuition and grow self-worth. You say clearly what you need. Saying you need some money (to pay your rent) may only get you bus fare or what others think you need. You don't ask a broke person for money. You don't give the keys to your house to a thief. You don't ask someone who is *never* on time to drive you to the emergency room. I have finally learned and stopped going to medical providers with any expectations that I'll receive anything close to services that support my health and well-being. I have been insulted, undiagnosed, misdiagnosed, and miseducated about my body. *"You're in your seventies. We can't give you new knees. Your skin is too thin. We can't remove thirty pounds of sagging skin from your 150-pound weight loss. African Americans' keloid."* These same doctors have been reluctant to prescribe pain medications for my pervasive arthritis and fibromyalgia or surgeries for the new knees, excess skin, hidradenitis suppurativa, and lipedema. My forty-five-dollar copay is better spent at a bingo hall.

Getting older brings humility and worrisome emotions. I've lived most of my life fearlessly. The list grows. I fear not being able to defend myself from physical violence. I have never been afraid of the police or being out alone at night or mindfully distrusting of most white people. "Kumbaya" is no longer on my playlist.

Getting old is universal. I have an agile mindset. I'm reaching for my highest level of human development. I'm at my tipping point.

I’ve reached my capacity for carrying grief. I’m at the pinnacle of sorrow. I have a big imagination, but my mind does not compute the gross social injustices, political fuckery, and inhumanity that’s running amok. It’s like trying to watch two movies at once, *Lord of the Flies* and *Deliverance.*

I believe I will exit peacefully. I hope my demise isn’t traumatic or a burden to my family and loved ones. I hope I have left a legacy for my family, friends, and communities. I wish to be revered as an Ancestor. And in the event that I don’t see great-grandchildren in this lifetime, I will return as a descendant. The family will gather to greet a newborn and exclaim, “They look like Iya! Iya has returned!” *Aṣe!*

At the Edge of the Cliff

GEORGIA A. GREELEY

I've always been there, we all are, it's just that now I can see the edge more clearly. One day I will step over that edge. Four of my friends have taken this step in the past year. But right now, I'm dancing along the edge. This is how I do it—I write.

Downsizing This Old Body

This old body
instigates
its own process;
Slows me down.
Insists on a wider view of life.
One part will stop working until I fix it,
which often means throwing
a part of a part away.

This process is more moth,
buried in spun silk, than butterfly,
hanging in an exoskeleton
exposed, transforming.

Yet unlike those winged creatures
my whole molecular structure

doesn't change.
I am still me with add-ons,
inner metals, and scars,
and a whole new world of
movement.

I can't fly like
those fragile hairy moths
but it's so very
close . . .

Things quit working. The nerves in your ears die. Joints need replacing. Your body moves and responds in new ways. You have to figure out how to live freshly with what still works and work around what doesn't. Moving may hurt. Not moving limits your life. What do you choose?

Oh, Mom

Jeanne Laurice Shillock 11/09/1927—06/29/2020

You taught me how to sew
and swear
You taught me how to cook
and pout
You taught me things
I never realized
until I started acting out.

You broke one promise
I was angry about
for years and years—
You *did not* send me
to a convent in Alaska when

I came home from college
talking about getting married
“before I was twenty-one.”
Damn.

But showing me how to die,
that made up for all of it.
I watched you let go
one part of your life after another
with joy
with relief
with gratitude
until all that was left
was this kind gentle being
I had not seen since I was a child.

Your last huge worry
was that you wouldn’t live
long enough
to say goodbye to
your youngest child,
who had to come from California.

You did last, though.
You were always stubborn.

He stayed a week,
you rallied,
felt well enough to start worrying . . .

Roy left.
And then you left,
dying three days later,
all worries gone.

I watched my mother let go as she lay dying. She seemed both relieved and happy. Mom became this spiritual bubble of body and happiness. I've found myself unconsciously trying on that kind of deep letting go. It scared me. It surprised me. It felt good. I found it rather seductive. I don't think I will be afraid of death when it comes. I'm definitely past midlife. We'll see what happens tomorrow.

Living/Outliving

after Adam Zagajewski

The wood outhouse stands, the concrete buddha sits,
trees line the two-rut dirt road like sentinels,
birds grouse and wait for me to leave.

My forest is never quiet—
flora and fauna creak and moan.

This lively land will still be here
when I've decreased to moisture, mud, and mound.

Alive and Singing

MARY MOORE EASTER

I

It was the Zoom panel by Gris Literature on old age and poetry that sent me to the computer, many months after the fact. My outrage was triggered by the moderator's questions and suggestions for our coming conversation. My newly repaired heart jolted at the approach. All seven of the preparatory questions contained the word "death." All seven! Apparently, one could only think about poems in old age if the context was the end of everything. The suggestions assumed our eminent decease.

Once the panel was in progress, I tried to correct this approach, interrupting every mournful story with lively protest. I'm sure I must have seemed unsympathetic at the very least, a kind of Pollyanna with a "yes, but" to those suffering heartbreaking losses, and the doom of factual crises ending their accounts of decline. But every "yes, but" had an insistent counterstory.

The alternate view came out of my own experience of open-heart surgery.

Before the actual operation, nurses and doctors asked me what goals I had. I guess they were trying to refocus my mind on the future—would there be one? They wanted to know where I wanted to get after open heart. Who would I be? What could I continue to do?

Of course I didn't say, "I'll return to all my activities without a break." What idiot would assume such continuity after the opening of my body cavity to replace the aortic valve (tired, worn out) and excise my aneurysm? Nobody asked about the inevitability of death. They didn't seem to think death was inevitable. With removal of the aneurysm, we'd already bypassed that possibility. I was already safe from instant death. That's why they were going to all this trouble. They were planning on life, continuity. They were earnest in their questioning. I started a quick review of what made living so urgent I could argue for it. In that leaping mind from thing to thing combined with the dangers of this surgery, a twofer—I asked if I'd be able to sing, a surprise to the nurse and doctor. The incision was near my lungs, all sorts of connections between heart and lungs. They noted it down for the coming rehab: *Wants to be able to sing.* It went without saying that as a dancer I wanted to be able to dance, not the way I used to when I was young. I'd given that up years ago, *learned* to give it up for the sake of reasonableness and care of my knees, and ankles, and the loss of my amazing jump. So that wasn't on the list of things I wanted back, not officially anyway.

The religious philosopher Howard Thurman once said, "When we sing, we praise twice."

That quotation struck me as so true. And that "we" made its truth mine, so much a part of the group whose song was created to rejoice, to pour forth something of personal value to the spirit and the world. I knew he was talking about African Americans. I didn't have to separate the two acts. Singing and praising were one and the same. And no cut through the cavity of my body was going to take it away from me. I didn't know then that part of my recovery would fall on my own shoulders. I was *required* to clear my lungs several times a day. They even gave me a heart pillow to ease the disturbance in my coughing chest. I now see them all over for people who need a way to brace the pain, not particularly to sing. You have to do it and medicine offers a way to do it. I had no idea that my goal of singing would follow me throughout my recovery. In the hospital I welcomed visitors, my pastor, Victoria, and my soprano friend Lynne, both of whom had witnessed me through the wait before surgery. My daughter Allison made up the 6:30 a.m. group. We prayed, sang, and quieted ourselves for a six-hour delay until the moment arrived. Singing was a part of our wait, praising, too, all in one. Allison improvises the alto to "This Little Light of Mine." At this point in my "faith journey" as I've learned to describe my path, I wouldn't have offered spiritual belief as foremost in my description of myself. But there it was innately combined in one act. I look back and acknowledge the deep spiritual merge.

Despite the length of remembering, it didn't take long to achieve the singing. I was still hooked up to tubes and chest drains when Pastor Victoria visited with Lynne. We were all members of the church choir and we started quietly singing a hymn, more than humming. As we progressed I thought of a spiritual I was sure they didn't know and I busted out with

> Mary *had* a little baby,
> born in *Beth*lehem.
> Every *time* the little baby cried,
> she rocked him in a *weary* land.

They didn't know to join in at the chorus, so I sang on alone:

> Ain't that *rock*in for the world
> Ain't that *rock*in for the world
> Ain't that *rock*in for the world
> Oh, she *rock*ed and *rock*ed.
> She *rock*ed him in a *wea-ry* land.

They exclaim. The phlegm in my lungs didn't impede me. I take deep breaths and belt out the birth of Jesus in a manger. Second verse comes. I know the story. I have sung full-throated, bustin those syncopations and offbeats in rockin' rhythm. Goal accomplished. Alive and singing.

II

Weeks later, free of tangled chest tubes and thoracic drains. And with several independent hallway walks under my belt, I show up at Cardiac Rehab. A new adventure. Will I be able to do what they ask? The nurse has a card with my post-surgery goals. "You want to sing?" "Well, yes. I already have." And I tell her the story of the spiritual in the hospital bed. We establish new goals. I want the walking machines. She sets up the treadmill, me attached by electrodes to measure my blood pressure, my effort. Keep the BP low, keep the effort steady, gain strength each day. I am the subject of praise and encouragement. All who come to our rehab group are focused on living, continuing to live. (I stick out my tongue at the death-promoting old age poets.) Privacy law keeps their conditions private, but they are free to tell us their ordeals and they chat. It's all about (1) the walk they achieved today, (2) the race they plan to enter, (3) the reacquisition of horseback riding skills for a former cowboy. He swings a leg over the saddle of a stationary bike to get started. The woman with my name is scared on the treadmill and creeps as if it would drop her through space if she trusted it on each step. My nurse says some people have trouble with the coordination. I can't help trying to show her that by swinging each leg forward, the treadmill will be there to accept her step. To keep walking interesting I hum a little rhythm under my breath, sort of dancing inside my body on the treadmill. I want that, too. First, I want the elliptical. That's the first time anyone has cautioned that I'm not ready for the exertion it requires. It's like a gauntlet thrown down. What do I have to do to get ready? Gradual progress is a definition of the dance training that is the story of my life. I work on the treadmill to reach greater consistent effort. I monitor the numbers on the machine. I have a new goal and I'm moving toward it.

Voltaire, Freud, and Me

CHRIS CINQUE

Often, in the middle of the night, I wonder how I will die. These thoughts have the same low-level intensity as when I think about what I might eat for breakfast the next morning. I'm curious and feel a tiny endorphic bump. Then I drift back to sleep.

I read once that Sigmund Freud fainted when he thought about his own death. Maybe this was a regular occurrence on his part, maybe the story is apocryphal, but I find it a startling response to this thing we all have in common, that one day we will die.

Dying is not a dominant concern in my life as I age, but I am curious about it. This wasn't always the case. I used to be afraid of dying when I was a child, subjected to the terrors taught me by the catholic church regarding sin and damnation. But I was a good child, more sinned against than sinning. Forced to examine my conscience starting when I was seven and confess my "sins" to whatever possibly predatory priest was on the other side of the curtained grill, I was caught in the grip of patriarchal hypocrisy. I worked hard at enumerating my sins, stretching my tiny transgressions into material worthy of the hushed confessional, taking my penances willingly as bulwark against the horrors of hell. Any sexual feelings that arose in me I squashed into numbness to save myself from eternal damnation. Any childhood rebelliousness was crushed by my fears of dying while in a state of sin. Maybe this is why Freud fainted over his own dying, maybe he was afraid of being dragged into hell for all the lies he told about women and our "neuroses," our penis envy and our desires to seduce our fathers and our relentless, intractable hysteria, all the smoke and mirrors he created when he himself knew that women's distress was caused by incest, other kinds of rape, and patriarchal oppression so smothering that women become unhinged.

Throughout my childhood I was subjected to sexual assaults by my mother's younger brother, a damaged man, alcoholic, orphaned at age seven when his mother died and his father abandoned him, a child, then a man, mostly unloved by the world in which he found himself. Whatever dynamic existed between him and his critical older sister, my mother, he exacted his revenge against his unhappy place in the world on me, his niece. At least that's what I think. Or he might simply have been so unable to express any personal agency that he turned to a child to assert his power. Whether he harmed other children as well I will never know, but child sexual abuse is extremely common. One in four girl children are subjected to sexual assault. One in thirteen boy children. This epidemic goes largely untreated and mostly unnoticed except by those suffering from its lifelong effects.

I didn't remember my uncle's assaults until I was in my sixties, but my life was full of distress as a result of them: depression, anxiety, fear of being away from home, addiction, insomnia, an abusive relationship, and a fifteen-year-long misdiagnosis of MS, all the result of complex PTSD caused by being attacked when I was not quite two, not quite four, six, eight, fourteen, and nineteen years old. So now, far along in my recovery from the horrors of my childhood, when I wake in the middle of the night and wonder how I'll die, I don't faint, I don't panic. I just go back to sleep.

I remember incidents of existential fear in my young adulthood. Alone in my second-floor apartment, dreading sleep, I would barricade myself in my bedroom. But then, no! Using tall ladders they will come in through the window and I won't be able to get out because I've blocked the door! I would stay awake all night terrified.

Or the time I was at a cabin in the woods, electric with fear being so far from home, the loons wailing on the lake and the gentle snoring of my partner and our dog sleeping obliviously near me. Another time, while trying to escape Minnesota winter, my wife and I went to San Diego. I couldn't sleep, imagining the polar vortex back home freezing the pipes in our house, which then burst, flooding the electrical system and causing an explosive fire burning down the house. After the second night of this, I asked myself with exasperation, Why am I so terrified? I got a clear response: "Bad things happen when you leave home." Well, I thought, that makes sense. All my sexual assaults but one happened away from home. The Italian proverb I grew up with says clearly: "Your mother's house is safe, warm, golden. Outside is danger. The wolf is there." My fears were not about dying, but about being overwhelmed again by forces beyond my control.

I came out as a lesbian in a small town in the South when I was nineteen, a few months after the Stonewall riots. The amount of homophobia I experienced devastated my highly sensitive self. I interpreted looks and comments, however harmless in their intent—though they were certainly not always that—as assaults on my humanity. Still, I pursued my life as a lesbian. I could do nothing else. I was what I was. I am what I am. However, the ostracization I experienced from my religion, my family, my community, and myself was so great I used to say that however I die, homophobia will have killed me. It takes a toll living with daily oppression, the micro cuts of mini aggressions, the macro cuts of assault and contempt, and the myriad forms that discrimination takes. So when I think about my death, it seems it might be a relief from pain rather than something to dread.

This is not to say my life has been an unrelenting series of unhappy events. I am devoted to my marriage and my amazing wife. By luck, I own a house that is beautiful and warm. I have had three careers—theater, teaching, and visual art—that have afforded me opportunities to express myself and be of service to others. I belong to a wonderful community of recovering addicts. I have many friends. I have fantastic physical health. I appreciate nature and find solace in being near water, especially the North Shore of Lake Superior. Though I lived on the financial edge most of my adult life, I was able to retire when I turned sixty-five. My days belong to me, free of money worries and full of opportunities to make art. What's not to love about life? Why am I *not* dismayed by dying?

When I look at the long arc of what we know about the history of human life on earth, I see endless war and suffering, the nonstop abuse of women and children, the horrors of racism and genocide, the endless cruelties perpetrated by patriarchal religions. This is not a world made for most of us. Patriarchy must be endured since we can only change it incrementally. In order to survive, we have to pretend that this affliction of male domination doesn't have the impact that it actually does. Our lives, our freedom, our communities, our sense of self are in constant conflict with this overarching misogynistic power.

In 1755, Voltaire wrote about the earthquake that struck Lisbon, killing tens of thousands of people. Voltaire didn't experience it directly, but reading about it and the suffering that ensued caused him such distress that it altered his life forever. One earthquake, one tragedy shattered his life, transforming him into the lifelong pessimist who wrote *Candide,* set in Lisbon, post-earthquake. I don't know what he thought of his own death before or after this event, but he said this about how to live: "The safest course is to do nothing against one's conscience. With this secret, we can enjoy life and have nothing to fear from death." Freud might have done well to follow his advice.

Voltaire died before the French Revolution. Given how devastating he found the earthquake, would he have survived emotionally the horrors of that catastrophic time? I think of all we know currently about the dreadfulness of living under mostly male rule and its warmongering; what easy access we have to the most cataclysmic stories; how familiar we are with genocide, slavery, holocausts, rape culture, oppressions of myriad kinds, famines, and other man-made catastrophes. Then there are the events like those Voltaire read about: earthquakes, forest fires, tsunamis, tornadoes, hurricanes, floods. I have to work hard—and I am by no means unique in this regard—not to be overwhelmed on a regular basis. I don't have much capacity to forget the things I already know, though I've gotten better at screening out the everyday onslaught of bad news. When the first terrible famine that I became aware of occurred in Ethiopia in the 1980s I wanted to die every day. I couldn't unsee the bloated bellies of the children or the helpless sorrow of their mothers. I was frantic to make a difference, to save somebody, anybody. But I had no clue as to how to make any kind of impact. And so awash in my own trauma-induced dysfunction, I was incapable of doing anything useful for others regarding issues as complicated as famine. As I got older, I learned to do what I could, to avoid the hubris of the savior complex, and be as content as possible knowing I'm not capable of or responsible for solving the world's problems. I try to do the best I can with what skills I have to effect changes closer to home and to do nothing against my own conscience. But is that enough? I don't know. But by dedicating myself to recovering from PTSD and living simply and purposefully, I have become highly functional and now have the energy to live what I hope is a useful life.

I'm an artist and art has saved my life. I believe that literally. I used to draw and paint as a child. Having access to that creative part of myself gave me courage and peace and a sense of self, counterbalances to the traumas I was experiencing. Creating involves making choices and taking action, which I couldn't do when being assaulted. Drawing connected me to myself and to others. As I grew up, I found other ways to express my creativity. I studied piano and taught myself to read orchestral scores so I could follow the music I loved. Then I chose theater as a way to combine all these elements into one. I wrote plays, acted, and directed. There was always a musical component to my plays as well as a marked physicality. They were rambunctious, funny, and exhilarating. There were times of transcendence doing this work, but I was often haunted by feelings of inadequacy and a sense of being a fraud. What difference was I making in the world? I know now that by being creative, I was saving my own life from a bottomless despair. And I was connecting with others. I was carrying messages of hope that were meaningful to many in the audiences who saw my work. This is the opposite of the loneliness and helplessness of being victimized by my uncle. Creativity is life affirming.

As an artist retired from having to work for anybody else, my days belong to me, all twenty-four hours. Every day is Saturday, my favorite day when I was somebody's employee. Now, as a visual artist, I'm doing work that brings me acceptance, engagement, happiness, and sometimes financial reward. I make abstract and figurative collages. I also draw and paint. In my abstract work, I stack blocks of color and texture. I find it soothing and meditative. My intention is to find places that are beyond words, beyond the strife of everyday life, free of the burdens of history, places of focus in a chaotic world. I try to communicate peacefulness and hope. I also make art that is overtly political, but my true joy lies in abstraction.

I get to make art every day. This is a happy place to live, like the reward of heaven promised by monotheistic religions after living in the hellishness that men have made of earth. But I don't have to die to reach some such mythical place. I can find peace within myself, with my wonderful wife, and with my friends.

Besides, I don't believe in god. I am not religious in any way, except for the indelible imprints made on my psyche by the indoctrination I was subjected to when I was too young to question or resist. But as an adult, I reject any notions of a personified god, benevolent or otherwise. I understand the desire for this, but while teaching people to love one another is a wonderful aspiration, the dogmas surrounding religion are deceiving and manipulative. I do believe in our capacity to love and experience the spiritually inexplicable. I believe in connections to others, to nature, and to art. I also, oddly, am an optimist. I believe humans are capable of solving every single problem that confronts us and that we might eventually figure it all out. I don't expect this to happen in my lifetime, of course, but we have moved often in the right direction over many excruciating eras. Young people are aghast as I once was at the state of the world. People claim that these are absolutely the worst of times. But the world has always been a dreadful place for most people. Yet we continue, inch by painstaking inch, to make progress. We continue to explore what it means to be our best selves. We continue to advocate for the most vulnerable, the most damaged, and the most misunderstood. Eventually, if we survive this sixth extinction of climate collapse, we could achieve nirvana. I get that that's a big if.

This essay started out as an exploration of my relationship to my own death. I continue to feel sanguine about that occurrence. The *New York Times Magazine* published an article called "What Deathbed Visions Teach Us About Living" (March 12, 2024). It said that some people have claimed that "deathbed visions are real, can provide comfort, *even heal past trauma*. That they can, in some cases, feel transcendent. That our minds are capable of conjuring images that help us, at the end, make sense of our lives" (italics mine). Who, when their time comes, wouldn't welcome such an event?

Older/Wiser/Older

DEBORAH KEENAN

We do have work: as cartographers
drafting maps of the wasteland
between health and death . . .

—Connie Wanek, "Brave Rabbits"

The various stories of growing older are claimed, dismissed, applauded, laughed at, disdained, or turned to holy writ, depending on one's point of view through the various lenses of spiritual life, emotional strength, physical health, financial safety (or lack of), race, gender, class, and physical appearance—so many more, of course, since we shape our lenses from the day we are born.

A key lens in my life as a creative human person are all the quotations I search for and save from thinkers, visual artists, musicians, and writers, especially poets, since I committed to the life of a poet at age nineteen and never looked back.

Stanley Kunitz wrote in his poem "Passing Through": *Don't take it so to heart. / Maybe I enjoy not-being as much / as being who I am. Maybe / it's time for me to practice / growing old.* And William Stafford wrote in his poem "Ask Me": *Sometime when the river is ice ask me / mistakes I have made. Ask me whether / what I have done is my life.*

So I ask myself, Is what I have done my life? Are my many books my life? My many collages? Are the readings I have given by myself or with others my life? Is one failed marriage, years of being a single parent, a lucky and sustained long second marriage my life? Are my beautiful grown children, all doing extraordinary good in the world, my life? Do I place my creative self, which burns still within me, on a higher pedestal than all my years of earning a living at my wild variety of jobs? Do I place my ability, my will, my desire to stay a creative person alongside my ability to take care of friendships, to honor my elders, to, as a beloved student once told me (in the hallway outside our graduate class, where points of view clashed with such intensity), *Don't worry, Deborah. we all have to learn/change/grow, and sometimes it has to happen in a writing class,* or do I secretly place one way I live over all the other ways I live? I still think about all of this, in my seventies. Lucy Sante wrote, with such brilliance, *We may have all stopped smoking, but we continue to burn.* I ask myself, In what ways do I continue to burn for art's sake? (and yes, I know, smokers still gather happily outside the institutions of protected air, my lost comrades). Do I still see everything in the world as a poem, as I did throughout my twenties? No. But I write the poems I must write. I am not interested in writing light poems, merely clever poems, though I am still deeply interested in how funny I find myself (at times)—the same is true with my collage work: If I must make one, I do. I have been fortunate to handle my own melancholy, to not be drawn to suicide as my father was; I have been fortunate to not live with chronic physical pain. Because these two things are true of my personal life, I am privileged to still live a creative life. And when I am sick of myself in particular ways, which I have written about in some of my books, it is because my privilege, my luck, the color I was born, those are the times when my sense of personal creating, its meaning or value, slips away for a time, and I bring up all the other lenses I see my life through, and try to do those parts with honor and attention. And yes, through those times I do long for my respect of my own creative life to return, and yes, thus far, it has. And I am grateful for that energy, that belief in self to return.

Adrienne Rich wrote, in "An Atlas of the Difficult World": *You are reading this poem through your failing sight, the thick / lens enlarging these letters beyond all meaning yet you read on / because even the alphabet is precious.* And C. D. Wright wrote: *Poetry is the language of intensity. Because we are all going to die, an expression of intensity is justified.* As an always intense human being, I am at peace with my intensity about making art, about all the wickedness loose in the world, about being overwhelmed by beauty—I feel justified.

Ask me if what I have done is my life . . . My answer today is mostly yes, though, sadly, if the answer is yes I have to count all the failures of love and attention, I have to own the good mistakes, and the lousy ones. But today I am clear that means I also get to own my striving as a creative person, to add something worth adding to this abundant world, I get to count that, too. And the name of this essay, "Older/Wiser/Older," I certainly claim older—it's shocking to be older. As I said to a dearest friend, if you don't die young, life is really long. I sometimes claim wiser. And all the parts of my life have led me to whatever wisdom I possess, and the still burning creative spirit in me has given me part of my wisdom here in my time on earth.

Parallax

A New Syllogism

MORGAN GRAYCE WILLOW

Summer nights on the farm where I grew up, thick clusters of stars filled the night sky in varying formations. We had a single yard light, and that could be turned off, opening up the night sky to us. Standing in the vast, dark space between the house and the barn, I learned to identify Ursa Major, Ursa Minor, the North Star, Orion, the Pleiades, which we called the Seven Sisters. The Milky Way was a vast smear of light clusters, bright spots, and star clouds. In August, the meteor showers performed streaks against a light-bedecked backdrop. I don't know if in all that star gazing I figured it out on my own, or if an older brother taught me, but if I looked at the North Star with my right eye covered, it appeared to be in the center of the sky. Then when I switched and covered my left eye, our lodestar appeared to have shifted eastward in the night sky. Later in seventh-grade science class, I learned that this phenomenon is called a parallax: "A change in the apparent position of an object . . . caused by a change in the observer's line of sight" (*American Heritage Dictionary Online*). I find that aging is like that. The vantage point from which we consider aging changes what we see.

To some, I have never "looked my age." When I was growing up, come Easter Sunday after mass my sister and I would stand on the broad expanse of steps in front of St. Peter's Catholic Church. Adults—usually great-aunts, second or third cousins—would come up to us, admire our hats, then follow those remarks with "Why you must be Ruby and Luvern's girls." After which they would turn to my sister, then as now two and a half years younger than me, and say, "You must be the older one." I was taken aback at age eight; I felt stripped of my due as the elder sister. By the time we were teenagers and had moved to a new parish—a mere clapboard building instead of an imposing limestone one, only three steps and no expanse at all—the remark was a full-on affront. I was the sister who already had a driver's license. I the senior in high school; she the freshman. In just one year, I would be off to college while she would remain in the small-town school and parish for four more years. After we, respectfully, corrected those adults, they would often respond with a chuckle and a remark such as "One day you'll be glad to be mistaken for the younger sister."

I didn't then, and honestly don't now, understand what it was about my sister's appearance that designated her "the older girl" in their minds. What was that "older look" she had that I wanted when I was eight or sixteen? What is the "younger look" I supposedly have now that should please me so much? What, after all, does any age "look like," whether it's twenty-seven, thirty-two, forty-five, fifty-nine, sixty-seven, or eighty-three? I bristle when someone says to me, "But you don't *look* seventy-five." "But," I'm tempted to ask, "just what does seventy-five look like?"

I'm sure most folks believe it's a compliment to tell me I don't look my age. In the moment of utterance, they're not cognizant that it presumes looking younger is always better than looking older. That is, after all, the message that dominates our media-driven culture.

Still, I feel I've earned the years I've lived, as well as how those years have written themselves on my face and body. I claim them as my own and do not wish to be stripped of them by someone else's supposed compliments. It seems to me their own discomfort with the aging process reveals itself in those remarks that deny my age. Or perhaps it's simply that the language we have immediately available in such situations is based on a fundamental judgment that aging is de facto a bad thing. It seems to me what we need, at the very least, is a different logical framework in order to shift our vantage point. We need a new syllogism to buttress language less fraught with negative connotations for aging. I suggest the following:

> Major Premise: This is what I look like.
> Minor Premise: I am seventy-five years old.
> Conclusion: This *is* what seventy-five looks like.

Or maybe it's not so new. As Gloria Steinem famously said, after being complimented by a reporter that she didn't "look forty": "This is what forty looks like." She has continued claiming her age, along with her look, as each decade has passed, including in March 2024, when she turned ninety. This, then, is what ninety "looks like."

All of this is not to say that I sail blithely into aging. Quite the contrary. I am susceptible to the dominant culture's prevailing attitudes, like everyone else. When I was young, I longed to be sixteen so I could get my driver's license and gain more autonomy through freedom of mobility. Then I looked forward to graduating and being out on my own, which meant being a first-generation college student. After having been so successful in high school, I felt young again, ill prepared as I was for the four-year liberal arts college environment. College was a culture and lifestyle no one in my family had experienced. Plus, it was all happening in the midst of the Vietnam War when friends were being drafted and swept away from the quiet order of the Iowa cornfields around us to the chaos of warfare and death in Southeast Asia. I felt naive and too young for my surroundings, yet at the same time grief stricken and old as I learned more about what was going on in the world around me. By the summer of 1968, after the assassinations of Dr. Martin Luther King Jr. and Robert Kennedy, the concept of aging into adulthood had lost its luster. My vantage point had shifted radically, changing my attitudes and beliefs about aging along with it. It felt to me that in certain ways, none of us in my generation were young anymore.

Fast-forward fifty years. Yes, fifty years. I'm stunned by how often in conversation I find myself saying that I've witnessed something that happened fifty years ago. Or that I've known someone or been involved with a group for fifty years. From the vantage point of seventy-five looking back, time feels so laden with personal and international crisis. I received a breast cancer diagnosis, for example, and needed to have a lumpectomy—which, fortunately, was successful. The election of 2016 happened, ushering in a period in American politics worse than anything I could have imagined in 1968. The election of 2024 left me speechless and sleepless.

Through most of those years, I have been using journals and notebooks to keep my writing life alive. In 2016, I attended a workshop with Naomi Shihab Nye in which she suggested that we give ourselves five to seven minutes of writing time first thing each morning, before the clutter and outside language of the world can get to us. We're certainly free to take more time if our day allows, but the daily gift of five to seven minutes can help us stay in touch with our inner lives and the interior language that goes with it. I've continued this practice. After pouring my first cup of coffee, I retire to my study, where I open what I call my Five to Seven notebook. This is a poetry notebook. I may or may not get a poem—or what I call a "jam"—on any given day, but I show up. Note the date and time. Then, usually, I jot "to journal" and turn to my journal where I record and reflect on the previous day's events and activities. Much of this is chronicling and processing the livingness of life. Most never makes its way into manuscripts. It does, however, clear the way for manuscript work. I've devised a system of indexing as I go so that I can retrieve information I think I may need for a manuscript. The notebooks and the journals complement each other. Notebooks are dedicated to creative work, which may be poetry, essay, or collage, while the journals help steady me through my days. I've shared this practice with students over the years, including in a class at the Loft Literary Center in Minneapolis called "Notebook to Manuscript." One consequence of all these mornings is that I have an entire closet brimming with boxes and shelves of journals, notebooks, and ephemera from a writer's life. Aging does have this, possibly questionable, side effect as well: accumulation. From my vantage point at seventy-five, the question that reverberates in my head is no longer "Who am I becoming?" but rather "What am I ready to let go of?" And that question is swiftly accompanied by "What am I going to do with all these notebooks and journals?"

About aging, Mickey Spillane said—and here I take liberties with Spillane's pronouns—"If you're a singer, you lose your voice. A baseball player loses her arm. A writer gets more knowledge, and if she's good, the older she gets, the better she writes." I want this to be true, though I know there is no direct corollary between knowledge and writing skill. Greater knowledge may simply require greater skill and hence demand more writing time to hone that skill. However, I often feel that the older I get, the less I know. On those days, it seems the world has become a less familiar place. Less civility. Less compassion. This requires of us that we examine the language we use to express the world we find ourselves in. And so it is with age and aging. If we don't want to be declared looking some other age than the one we are, it's going to be up to us to name it. We need to stake a claim to our line of sight, and declare, in language that's adequate for the age we are and how we look, our own vantage point. To shift the parallax on aging.

Finding My Way

KATHRYN HADDAD

When I was in sixth grade, I had a lot of anxiety about entering junior high the next year. I had no older siblings and didn't know anything about what it would be like, except for what I had seen on television. I had grown up watching *The Brady Bunch* in reruns and had seen Marcia and Jan in their junior high, and that was my only frame of reference. The colorful miniskirts and maxi boots that came up to the knee that they wore were so cute—but nowhere to be found in the mall by my house or at Target, where we usually shopped. I was afraid to go to school and look different from all the other kids. I didn't really consider the fact that the show I had been watching was in reruns and was filmed several years earlier when the fashions were different, and that Marcia and Jan's school in Southern California was probably different from mine in Minnesota, like much of their life was. But I fretted over the fact that I did not have the clothes or hairstyle of the Bradys, and things in junior high would be difficult for me because of it.

I was relieved and (I must say) a little disappointed to find on the first day that the girls in my junior high looked just like the girls in my elementary school and dressed the same as I did. No one had miniskirts or knee-high boots. They had Levi corduroys and Nikes. In fact, they were mostly the same kids from sixth grade. Of course! I laughed at this disconnect and realized my mistake. This junior high was in my neighborhood, and a continuation of sixth grade actually. It was not so different at all. But no one had warned me or helped me or informed me about what it would be like to enter junior high. I eventually figured it out and ultimately trusted myself to do what I felt was best, and I had a great experience during those years.

I feel much the same about entering my "senior years." I have seen a lot of shows on television about people growing older and retiring. I have seen movies, read books, and even, of course, been around as my parents and grandparents have aged. Will I lose my mind like those old women in sad movies? Get some debilitating disease or condition that will prevent me from walking? Have nothing to do but sit in a chair all day? Do I have to cut my hair short and wear sensible clothing? What will it be like for me? Am I prepared? Will my life be like theirs?

I remember my grandmother from Lebanon arriving to our house at about the same time that I was ready to enter high school. She was in her mid-seventies, and there was a terrible war in Lebanon. She came to the United States for the first time as a refugee, and it was also the first time I had ever met her.

She was so different from the old people I had seen up to that point. She had long hair that went down to the middle of her back that she would wind up in a bun to the nape of her neck. She wore dresses and would crochet for hours on end sitting on the floor in the living room—rarely did she sit on a chair. She went out to the yard of our suburban house for hours during the day, and picked the "weeds" that were growing, chopped them up, fried them with onions and olive oil and added lemon and ate them. Sometimes she would even squat in the yard in her dress instead of coming into our house to use the bathroom. This image of old age was a great contrast to one that I had ever known at that time. She never learned English. She would sit by the window and cry, and hold her hands up to the sky, saying *"Libnan!"* as she mourned her lost life in the village.

My other grandmother (my mother's mother, who was born in and had grown up in the United States) lived in a senior citizen apartment in a suburb about twenty minutes away from us. We would visit her on Sundays, and sometimes I would stay with her on my holidays. I loved staying with this grandmother. She would cook Banquet fried chicken, cream of potato soup, baked beans, and get me my favorite dinner when I stayed there: Swanson frozen meals. We would walk up to "town" kicking rocks along the railroad tracks on the way, and go shopping together, or take the senior citizen bus on longer trips to the Eden Prairie Mall, where once I remember she bought me bubble gum ice cream at Bridgeman's and all the things that my mom and dad would never get me because they were too expensive or not practical. She even had a "gentleman caller" who lived down the hall and who would come over and watch *Lawrence Welk* with her every evening. This grandmother was very happy in her life. My grandfather had died several years earlier, and she had found a rich existence. People wondered why I liked to stay with her in that tiny one-bedroom apartment, but it was such a treat for me to live this different life and be with my grandmother. I was special and spoiled and I loved her.

My mother, on the other hand, is experiencing old age in a way that is very sad to me. She is not able to walk, and she is in an assisted living facility. Even though the facility has many activities and very nice older residents, she is not interested in participating, not interested in going to the dining hall with the other residents, but chooses to stay alone in her room and eat. She sits in her chair all day and is sad. She does not feel well, she says, and our attempts at helping her through many doctor visits, medications for her depression, and suggestions for some levity have not been successful. She has no interests—doesn't like movies or TV or books or music. She does puzzles on her phone and sleeps and tells us she does not feel well.

What will I be when I get to this age? How can I make my life one that is full of purpose and gives me joy and inspiration? I am different from all these women in that I have not had children, I have lived alone for much of my adult life, and I have created a rich existence as a community organizer and artist. I love music and movies and cultural activities. I want to write and play music and create things. I want to participate in the world as much as I can. I want to tell stories and laugh and love.

I have some things that none of these women had—a life as a single woman that I have carved out alone, one with a long history of community building and arts work locally and nationally. I have developed several groundbreaking local arts nonprofits that I have led for over three decades now, worked as a writer and teacher, amassed several awards and fellowships, and lived my life in my own way, sometimes wandering down paths that seemed scary and different from anyone's I had seen in my family. Where my mother's and grandmothers' years were spent tending to houses and husbands and children, mine were spent writing plays, organizing conferences, developing organizations, and traveling to places all over the world. I am the child of an immigrant father and a mother whose family came as European settlers a century ago. Neither here nor there, this nor that, I have had to figure it all out as I have gone on my way in life.

Will my books and my music and my desire to create continue to make my life rich as I go through the transition to old age? Will I be like one of my grandmothers or my mother? Or like the old ladies in movies and TV shows I have seen throughout the years? Is there a path to follow? I think back to the Bradys and laugh to think about what Marcia or Jan would do. But I know now that my life is different, and I will have to figure it out myself.

1966

Duluth, Minnesota

VENUS DE MARS

Summer

It's raining. But warm. Which is nice. I see steam rise off the asphalt-patched street. I look through our large front window.

It's been raining for days. And my six-year-old self is tired of it. Tired of being inside. Mom says it's okay to go out. If I dress for it. Which I can. It's just a light rain. No thunder. No lightning. Nothing like the lightning I watched crackle through an evening's black sky weeks ago with my cousin Chris.

That evening we stood in our front entryway and watched through the glass storm door. Counting. A-thousand-and-one, a-thousand-and-two, and on. Till thunder, following a flash, rumbled loud. My cousin said every "thousand" equals a mile. Told me that's where lightning hits.

I remember watching him. Arms outstretched. Slow sway-dancing. His face toward the black sky. Waiting. Softly chanting a singsong. Like a trance. Till the next flash of bright. He yells in a burst of excitement. Each time. Each flash-jagged pattern. His dancing wilder as we count the "thousands" together, till thunder pounds. Till thunder punches our chests. Knocks us laughing and hollering. The "thousands" becoming less and less till we can't count a single thousand before the crash about breaks our ears.

Mom closes the wood front door then. Tells us both to move to the living room. Which we do. Till it's flashes with just a distant rumble. Then, only flashes. Then, only rain.

This rain today is nothing like that. It's only a drizzle.

I pull my raincoat on. The yellow slicker. With buckles for buttons and a yellow visor and a buckle under my chin. Like a space helmet fastened.

I pull on boots. Hop down the steps. Walk toward the street with no one else around. I step off the curb and onto an asphalt patch. Jump from it to the next. Then the next. The rain steady. A quiet noise enveloping.

When I reach the other side, I see Melinda walk out her door. The only other person around. She lives across the street. She's a few years older. I've never talked with Melinda. Because I don't know her. And all my friends are boys. And boys are friends with boys. And girls are friends with girls. So, I don't know what to do when she waves hi. But there's no one else, so I wave hi back. She smiles and walks over.

She's wearing a raincoat too. Like my yellow slicker. Except hers has regular buttons, not buckles. And it's light pink. With big yellow-white flowers. Like daisies. She has a rain hat too. But not like a space helmet. It's just a hat. Her boots match her coat. Mine are just black with a yellow-stripe top.

She asks what I think of the rain. I say it's warm. *She* says it's pretty with the mist and steam. She says she likes the sound. The sprinkles and quiet. I listen again. Look again. She says she likes the smell. I notice the smell. It's like earth.

A car slowly drives down the hill. It passes, turns around the corner, then heads down the steep on Fifty-Fourth. We watch the rain move back into the tire-emptied holes. The broken cement spots. She points to a patch and says it looks like a diving board, the puddle around it a pool. I see it. A long asphalt patch halfway across a puddle. She tells a story about how *lovely the pool looks* and how *this must be the new diving board they've just installed.*

I'm unsure what to say when she asks if I agree. But I say, *Yes. That must be it.* We take turns walking down this *new diving board.* Jump into the puddle-pool.

Melinda asks what I think of the new fashions.

I'm silent. I have no idea what she means. But I pretend I do. Say something like *They're okay.* She says she likes the boots out now. And the miniskirts. Wishes she could cut her hair in bangs. Like actresses on TV.

And I understand. She means clothes. The clothes that girls wear. And the long hair that girls have. And I wish I could wear all that. And I wish I could grow my hair long. But I don't say this. Instead, I say, *My hair has bangs.* Which it does, but not like a girl's. My hair is short on the sides. She adds that she likes bangs like Agent 99's on the TV show *Get Smart.* I say I like Agent 99's bangs too. And I do. And it occurs to me then that I like them for the same reason Melinda does. She wishes she could cut her hair like Agent 99's. And so do I. But I don't say this.

I remember watching TV with my sister. Watching the go-go dancers on music shows. All tall and thin. In high white boots and shiny striped dresses. And they all wear bangs and long hair. And I want that too. The dresses. The long hair. The bangs. The boots.

Last Christmas I asked for green corduroy hip-hugger pants. Out of the Sears catalogue. With extra-wide ribs and a wide leather belt with a matching paisley shirt and a yellow silk neckerchief with a tiny brass ring for adjusting on my neck either left, or right. It was all English-mod. Like on TV.

That year I got those hip-hugger pants with the extra-wide ribs with the matching paisley shirt and the yellow neckerchief. And I loved them. I wore them all night. I couldn't wait to wear them to school after Christmas. I looked just like the English movies.

And I did wear them to school. After Christmas. The teacher said I looked smart. But the other kids didn't. They said I looked stupid and laughed. One whispered that I really shouldn't wear the neckerchief especially. I asked why. He said it made me look like a girl. I took it off and put it in my pocket. When I got home, I put the whole outfit away. I never wore it again.

Melinda and I stand on the boulevard. The rain still mostly drizzle. She points to the sky and tells me to look for rainbows. Says they must be up there somewhere. I look. Our heads tilt back. Rain hitting our eyes. Melinda says we should open our mouths to catch the drops. So we do. Till the drops fall too fast. And the clouds get too dark.

Melinda turns as the rain gets worse. Tells me we really must do this again. She uses her pretend voice. Says we could *visit the pool.* Maybe *wander the grounds.* I say okay. The rain falls harder. She smiles, then turns to run across the street. The rain is storming now. Melinda stops on the other side of the street, turns, and waves. I wave back. She runs to her house and goes inside.

As her door closes, I run to my house. I think to myself. I wish I could be like her. I wish I could be like Melinda.

Begin counting the thousands. Let's measure time. Let's measure distance. Let's count till thunder hits.

Be Old and Just Get On with It

DEBRA J STONE

Although I wrote in my journals, it wasn't until out of frustration with my acting career that I began to write with more intention in these journals. It allowed me to process my thoughts about the world I lived in. Later, I started a writing group with another writer and taking classes at the Loft. I didn't know if I'd ever become published, but I liked writing. So, after a while, my short stories, essays, and poetry became published in literary journals.

At seventy-two, I published my debut novel, *The House on Rondo.* People who don't know me were amazed at my age when they found out I authored a novel. I'm enjoying the process of publication. In my debut novel, I tell the story of Rondo Avenue, where my mother's family and their neighbors lived until its destruction. I write about the lives of working-class Black people in Minnesota, who are often overlooked in literature and deserve to have their stories told. My stories and characters are created like those of my favorite author, Zora Neale Hurston, who wrote about the country folks of the South. These were people Ms. Hurston knew and gave a place in the literary world.

In her book *Trace: Memory, History, Race, and the American Landscape,* Lauret Savoy writes about the disappearance of ancestors: "Ancestors disappeared—into paper records of property rather than human lives remembered in story, into a plantation owner's surname, into graves unmarked or forgotten long ago." Contrary to this, for Rondo, the vibrant Black community of St. Paul that flourished from the early 1900s to the mid-1960s, the records of property owned by Black citizens refused to be buried in government archives. There are storytellers, novels, documentaries, and parades celebrating the ancestors and descendants of the Rondo community.

Since retirement, I no longer make hurried scribbles before my nine-to-five job. I've never had daily practice; it doesn't work for me. There are days when I write with a sudden burst of ideas and thoughts simmering in my head. I think of writing as being integrated into all my life's passions. The writing retreats I've participated in are like delicious candy to devote all time to writing without the interruptions of daily life. I'm lucky to be chosen to attend some of these retreats. At times, the local library or camping trips provide me with go-to places for fewer interruptions, deeper reflection, and ideas.

All of this is to say, every person will have their own way of putting words on the page and decide for themselves about their writing life. I found this book on writing helpful by Carl Phillips, *My Trade Is Mystery: Seven Meditations from a Life in Writing.*

My mother was my champion and encouraged my writing. I think all writers, at least in the beginning, need someone who's on your side and gives you courage to go on with your writing. Thelma Price Stone, eighty-six years old, passed away in January 2016, from complications of breast cancer, a week before my sixty-fourth birthday. I'd like to think she didn't want me to forget her. How could I? I feel my mother's spirit, her laughter, her joy. Like rain clears the air, I let these feelings pass through me and let the ancestors' spirits help me shape the words I write.

I learned from my mother the importance of story. Her family members were alive with stories. I'm keeping those stories alive and telling a few of my own, like Grandpa Joe, Uncle Skeeter, Cousin Dottie, Auntie Jane, and my mother. Mother said family are the holders of sacred rememberings.

My mother didn't live long enough to read my published book. I know she'd have a good laugh. "You finally finished! I knew you'd write about the Sandhills of Nebraska. You put your grandpa's stories to good use."

This was the land third great-grandfather Turner homesteaded, a cattle ranch. When the ranch couldn't be sustained, the family migrated to Rondo Avenue.

I miss my mother's phone calls. If I wasn't home, she'd leave a message: "Hi, it's your mom." Like I wouldn't know her voice.

Be fearless would be the ancestors' voices . . .

I discovered in my genealogy research I'm the first-born daughter of a long line of first-born daughters. Mother was the first-born daughter, and her mother was a first-born daughter, and my great-grandmother was her mother's first-born daughter. The women on the maternal and paternal side of my family are all first-born daughters going back to the days after slavery ended. Before slavery, I do not know what happened to the daughters and women. Few records remain of the enslaved women in my family. I can only guess from European DNA what had happened. But I do know this: These Black women ancestors were creative subversives, finding ways to release their creativity within a racist, sexist society. No one told them how to think or act; they didn't try to imitate upper-class white or Black society.

Until the store owner refused to pay my aunt, she drew fashion illustrations for a Minneapolis women's department store; another aunt copied high fashion clothes with patterns she created by looking at garments in the Minneapolis and St. Paul department stores that refused to let Black women try on clothes. My women ancestors developed their own recipes, made up bedtime stories about John Henry for their children, strengthening and protecting them from the brainwashing racism of white fairy tales. They designed their own homes, performed in vaudeville theater; no one became famous but that didn't stop their creative spirits. I remember hearing their stories and seeing these Black women. They were like fire agates. Smooth, iridescent, tough like the gemstone, difficult at times to cut through to find softness. Women with reddish to deep-brown to pale-brown hues like the agates found by Lake Superior if you're lucky.

Be fearless be old and just get on with it . . .

My aging philosophy is simple: be old and just get on with it. I don't have any good advice. I'm lucky to have my health and be able-bodied to enjoy nature hikes with my husband and our dog, camping, and biking—he's healthy, too, so we can enjoy this together.

A June day with puff clouds and a blue cornflower sky. I'm like a heron flying along Theodore Wirth Parkway. Below is the sound of the gurgling Ȟaȟá Wakpádaŋ, wind whistling through my bicycle helmet, riding my e-bike, following the pathway of the Grand Rounds to Minnehaha Falls.

The next day I hear and feel my knees creaking like my closet door hinges in need of a squirt of WD-40 oil. Since I can't oil my knee joints, I pop into my mouth two Aleve pills and half a CBD gummy.

I keep learning; nothing stops me if I get out of my own way.

My fear of deep water was so bad I insisted on snorkeling in Key West only in water where my feet could touch the sandy bottom of the Gulf of Mexico. The snorkeling instructor was very kind and never said a word about my weirdness. I didn't go far. Later, in early fall, I went to Bde Maka Ska to paddleboard with my husband, and he said if I learned to swim he'd buy me a paddleboard with a life jacket. A week later, I enrolled in the YMCA swimming class, and at sixty-two, I learned to swim the front crawl and backstroke, and can tread water. I conquered my fear of deep water. Now I swim the entire length of the pool. But my husband hasn't bought me a paddleboard yet. I'll buy my own!

I have no children. I will have no inheritors. Who would want my journals of scribbles of first drafts of poems, short stories, unfinished novels, grocery lists, to-do lists, phone numbers, passwords to things that have no meaning, and published literary journals and a novel? What will become of my writing?

There was a newspaper account of the discovery of a writer's book in the Goodwill bin. It turned out to be worth millions of dollars at auction.

I imagine it is unlikely my book in the future will be worth millions. My wish is that Black women writers will not be forgotten and that our work will be recognized in the Black literary canon. Like my favorite author, Zora Neale Hurston. So maybe I should keep some of my writing stuff.

Questions We Didn't Ask

CAROLYN HOLBROOK

To my beloved son Steven LaMarre Holbrook.
You will live forever in my heart.

When I got the invitation to contribute an essay to this anthology, I didn't have a clue what to write about. All my life I've heard about the aches and pains associated with the aging body, the seemingly inevitable weight gain after menopause, about becoming invisible, being displaced and replaced by younger women in the workplace and our romantic lives, and, of course, about our mortality. I puzzled and puzzled for months. None of those topics appealed to me and I couldn't think of another one I wanted to consider. I also thought about writing about how aging has affected my writing. That didn't appeal to me either because, like anything else in life, I believe my writing has improved with age and continued practice.

Then one day shortly after returning from my granddaughter's graduation from an HBCU in Virginia, my youngest daughter, Ebony, mentioned the difficulties I'd had while we were navigating the airports; especially the Detroit airport where we'd had a layover on the way home. I remember walking down the ramp from the plane into the airport with my traveling companions, Ebony and her youngest, my granddaughter, Najah. We walked past lobbies where passengers waited for boarding calls, and the wide aisles where travelers moved about with their luggage, some strolling leisurely, others practically running in order to get to their gate on time. And I remember taking in the aroma of coffee and the smells of a variety of foods that wafted through the air, both greasy fast food and international cuisine.

All of a sudden I couldn't go any farther. Pain had settled into my thighs and I was having difficulty breathing due to the asthma I had slowly developed over the previous few years. I remember standing still, trying to catch my breath while staring helplessly at the moving walkway that was just far enough away to be out of reach, and looking up to see the bright red tram that seemed to float by on a track above my head carrying passengers from one part of the massive airport to another.

Soon, I heard Ebony's voice among the noises that populate an airport: the hum of people talking, small children laughing or crying, disembodied voices announcing boarding calls, luggage wheels rolling on the concrete floor alongside their owners' shoes; sneakers squeaking with every footfall or hard-soled shoes padding along step by step. And, of course, the tram that whooshed by every four or five minutes.

"I thought you were with us," Ebony said as she and my granddaughter took their places on either side of me like protective bodyguards.

I thought I heard a tinge of fear in her voice when she said that she and Najah were alarmed when they realized they had left me behind while they enjoyed a stroll through the airport.

They both looked at me with concern when I offered a weak apology for having held them up. Then they ushered me to an empty seat in the lobby that was closest to where we were standing. Najah asked if I'd be okay if they left for a few minutes to pick up snacks and coffee.

When they returned, they were accompanied by an airport employee who was pushing a wheelchair. I remember looking down to avoid the pitying glances that were sure to be on the faces of strangers who passed us while the kind young man rolled me to the gate where we would wait for our second flight, and thinking, "This is where I am now. This is what it has come to."

A month or so later, while I was relaxing comfortably in Ebony's beauty salon, she picked up where she had left off in the airport. While gently massaging my shoulders, she let on that our trip to Virginia was a wake-up call that showed her her mother is no longer the youthful, energetic spirit she once was. Then she went on to tell me that she and her siblings had been having conversations about how it feels to watch me age.

Boom! There it was—I had my topic!

As I listened to my beloved child, my thoughts reverted back to watching with terror and fascination as my own mother aged. It was as though one day she and my stepdad were all decked out for a night out on the town and the next day, while driving her to the Minneapolis office of Barack Obama's presidential campaign where she volunteered, I was shocked to notice for the first time that her hair had turned silver and her beautiful "high yellow" complexion that always reminded me of fresh peaches had become puffy and wrinkled. She was still enjoying an active life and was beaming with pride in the hope that America might elect its first Black president, yet it was terrifying to realize that she had become an elder citizen. I knew the change had developed gradually. Why did it seem so sudden to me? Hadn't I been watching her carefully enough? Had I taken my mother for granted, believing she would always be the elegant young woman who raised me?

Since my mother's death in 2013, my children and I have had many conversations where we puzzled over questions we wish we had asked her, questions we all know she would have answered had she known we had them. When we knew Mother's last days were drawing near, I was moved when my middle daughter, Tania, invited her to visit the charter school where she was employed at the time to give the students a glimpse of what her life was like when she was in middle school. Tania gave each of us a copy of the videotape she made to memorialize the visit so that we could hear "Granny's" voice anytime we wanted with a simple touch of a button on our devices. But at the time, none of us were aware of the questions we might have asked that we now wish we had the answers to.

In an effort to ensure that my five children will have as few lingering questions as possible when my expiration date arrives, I have offered them numerous invitations to ask questions they might have about me, my life, and even about mistakes I made in parenting them. My children are an amazing group of humans. They're smart and talented, and each one's capacity for caring and loving-kindness shines through in their individual personalities. Also, in this mother's biased eyes, my children and grandchildren are incredibly beautiful with their tall and lithe, or shorter, curvy frames and their skin tones that display the full range of the almond brown palette along with their long dreadlocked or short-cropped, neatly trimmed hair. And then there are their voices. Whether we're on the phone or at family gatherings I love to close my eyes and listen to their voices that range from the sound of tinkling bells to deep bass—all of the intonations you might hear in a well-trained choir.

I take tremendous pride in the trust my family and I share. They know they can talk with me and each other about anything that's in their hearts and on their minds, so I was surprised when none of them took me up on my offer except Tania, who has always been willing to ask the big and small questions that concern her.

Ebony's comment showed me that there might be a different way to think about my unanswered invitation. I decided to take the onus off them. Instead, I would be proactive. I would ask them the questions I think they might want answers to.

I had already scheduled a date with Stevie, my firstborn, when Ebony and I had our beauty salon conversation, so I decided to begin my new adventure with him. I wasn't sure how to broach the subject. After fumbling around in search of the right words, I ended up blurting it out, asked why he doesn't ask questions about things he might be curious about. His answer made it clear that my new approach was indeed the right one because the first thing he said was, "I don't ask questions because that would make it real."

Wow! Could that be a reason for some of the questions we had been reluctant to ask Granny while she was still here?

Stevie's demeanor changed as he continued to consider my question. His usual manner, which tends to exude dynamism and humor, suddenly became contemplative. The look on his handsome face became serious as he went on to tell me that the thought of me dying is too frightening to think about, so he does all he can to avoid it, often staying away from me so that he won't have to see my graying hair, witness my slower gait, and react to my need to ask him to repeat things, despite his booming bass voice, because my hearing isn't as strong as it used to be. His response also forced me to recall the times I sometimes wanted to avoid my mother for the same reasons, though I don't think I understood it back then. His answer also caused me to wonder if this might be what's behind the reason for complaints I've heard from friends whose family members, particularly their brothers, it seems, may not spend much time with their aging parents, leaving their responsible sisters frustrated and angry, and leaving their parents feeling like they've been forgotten.

Talking with Stevie and Ebony (my oldest and youngest) gave me a bit more courage to approach my other three kids. My lovely middle daughter, Tania, and I decided to stop for dinner on our way to a concert at the art school where she is the director of student life (aka vice principal). I had told her what was on my mind the week before, so she was ready when I popped the question.

"What is like for you to watch me age?" I asked after we placed our orders. I was full of confidence coupled with dread, knowing that Tania does not mince words.

"Mom, it's f'ing weird" were the words that spilled out of her mouth, almost unbidden. Clearly, she had been thinking about it.

Tania went on to tell me that it's mind-blowing to see my skin wrinkle in the same places that Granny's skin wrinkled and my hair grow thin in the same places that Granny's hair thinned. Then she went on to say, "You probably don't know how closely I watch you when we're together." And then after taking a bite of her burger she added, "It makes me want to let go of whatever mother issues I have and just enjoy you."

Our conversation moved to lighter topics while we enjoyed our meal, but we couldn't resist returning to the major subject between bites. At one point, a pensive look passed over her face and she said that my aging mostly makes her want to reminisce about the good and not-so-great times we've spent together, and about conversations we've shared over the years.

Her final words came while we were climbing back into her SUV after dinner. I watched my deeply caring daughter turn slightly away from me as she muttered, "Saying all of this out loud to you was weird." I didn't tell her that hearing it was also weird.

With each child, my interviewing skills improved and, of course, my conversation with each of them was different. My handsome second-born son, Julian, moved to Los Angeles several years ago, so we don't see each other as much as we used to. At least not in person. But thanks to FaceTime, text messaging, and good old-fashioned phone calls, we enjoy frequent laughter-filled and sometimes serious conversations that range from the music he's composing to the dollhouse my daughter-in-law, Debbie, is building for their granddaughter, to the poems he's been writing for their grandbaby, and anything else that just happens to come up.

Julian's response surprised me. He basically said that my aging hasn't affected him much. "I'm not in Minneapolis, so I don't see what my siblings see," he said in his deep, melodious voice. He went on to tell me that our conversations don't give him reason to be concerned. My mind seems sharp and our conversations have an easy flow. He doesn't know that I turn my better ear toward the phone when we're talking.

I guess I really shouldn't have been surprised. I know my sweet son well enough to understand that he feels things deeply, but he is a man of few words. The depth of his love and compassion is more likely to come through in the music he composes rather than the words he speaks. At the same time, he is a realist. No doubt he views my aging the same way he views his own and his wife's dance with life: that aging is a reality that we will all face if we live long enough.

My eldest daughter, Iris, was my final interview subject. It's been two years since she moved to Atlanta to be with her son and his family after he relocated to follow workplace opportunities. Last month, I enjoyed a road trip with my daughter Tania and granddaughters, Ebony's daughter, Najah, and Iris's daughter, Tess. It was a delightful trip. Lots of girl bonding on the way there and back, and lovely time with family while we were there. However, we were all aware that Tess wasn't feeling well. In fact, Iris, who hadn't seen her beloved daughter in a while, was alarmed by the frail, fragile way she looked.

On the day we left to return home to Minneapolis, my kind and gentle daughter sent her child off with tools intended to help keep her spirits up both physically, emotionally, and spiritually: a notebook filled with handwritten affirmations, and pens, pencils, colored pencils, and crayons so that Tess could spend time reflecting on them in whatever ways she chose to. But none of us knew what was about to happen.

A few days after we returned home, Tess ended up in the emergency room followed by three weeks in the hospital where she was diagnosed with a rare and difficult-to-diagnose autoimmune disorder. Iris immediately flew up from Atlanta and camped out in the hospital room with her child. It took a while but, thankfully, the doctors put together a viable treatment plan, and we are all keeping close watch as her health slowly improves.

I'm grateful that I was able to have my conversation with Iris sometime between the day I returned home from the road trip and the day she flew up to be with Tess in the hospital. The first thing she shared was how disturbing it was to see me walking with a cane after I'd had a hip replacement several years ago. She said her first thought was "Oh no! You're supposed to be around forever!" Granny's passing was a tremendous loss for all of us but especially for Iris. The two of them had a special bond. Now she has to think about the possibility of losing me as well.

She felt better when I healed quickly and wholly from the hip replacement, but it sparked a lingering thought: "Who am I going to call if you're not here?"

Though our conversation was on the phone, I could hear the wistfulness in her voice and imagined a look on her face that matched the tone of her voice when she said, "I'm running out of people to talk to" followed with a question of whether I might want to move to Georgia to be with her when the time comes. "It crosses my mind over and over," she said as we concluded our conversation.

Writing this essay and grappling with these questions has caused me to fall in love with my children and grandchildren all over again, which I tend to do frequently anyway. My belief in the strength, power, and necessity of intergenerational dialogue causes me to learn as much from them as I hope I am imparting to them. It has also caused me to discover that the thought that I won't be able to be with my beloved family someday fills me with dread. My hope is that the conversations I've opened up will spring the door even wider for more discussion. And even though I wish I'd never have to leave them, I hope there will be few lingering questions when we say "So long" for the last time.

Letting Go, Being, Becoming

REBECCA PAVLENKO

Life as an artist is marked by change and impermanence. When I was studying to be a photographer, learning how to develop film and print images in the darkroom, there was a lot of emphasis on archival processing to make images permanent so that they wouldn't fade over time. Even though I followed all the steps—carefully mixing the chemicals in the correct ratios, washing prints the requisite amount—there were still times when the images would fade anyway! What does it mean to make something permanent? Can that ever really be done? Even with all the chemistry possible, everything changes. I noticed impermanence most markedly when the photography world went digital and everyone started carrying cameras disguised as phones. Suddenly many of the supplies I had carefully tested and selected started disappearing; they were no longer being made. I would get together with other photographers and we would mourn the loss of favorite photo papers. Oh, how I missed the lush, warm tones of Agfa Portriga that made images look like they were printed on parchment paper.

One of my main photographic projects involved photographing Japanese gardens, which I did for over fifteen years. Each time I went to a familiar garden, it would be different, changed. The lilacs were no longer blooming, but the iris were. Other plants were just budding out. It changed the focal point of the view each time I was there. I was photographing time, change, the cycles of impermanence. I made

Polaroid transfer images, which were made by projecting a color slide onto Polaroid film and then peeling the film apart and pressing the image into watercolor paper. It made for a delicate, almost painterly image with uneven edges. They were quiet, soft images that reflected the feel of the gardens. But, to my dismay, Polaroid went out of business. I bought up all the Polaroid film I could afford, and then my project was forced to come to an end when I used up all the film. The materials of my craft were no longer being made. I could no longer make those images.

I eventually switched to doing digital photography, which was like learning to write in a different language, with different syntax and more complicated grammar rules. At the time I felt like my lover had died and I was being forced to date someone who I wasn't even sure I liked. But eventually I grew to discover ways to expand my photographic thinking through the new techniques that digital photography afforded. We became friends, and now working digitally is part of my creative life.

While I did photography for my own expression, for fourteen years my day job was as a scenic artist for the Guthrie Theater. I was part of a team that sculpted, textured, and mostly painted the sets, floors, furniture, backdrops, and anything else that was on stage for the plays. Often we would work for weeks on a single thing, such as hand-stenciled, intricate wallpaper that took many steps. When finished, we would then have to paste it to the walls of the flats. The scene with that wallpaper might last only twenty minutes. The entire run of the show could be measured in weeks and then all our work was gone, either recycled, trashed, or given away. I remember watching the Tibetan monks who came to the Minneapolis Institute of Art create a mandala. They worked with utter concentration, devotion, and care to make an intricate, gorgeous mandala from colored sand that would be swept into a river, washed away, and let go. It was a lesson in impermanence that taught me to do my best, even with something that wasn't going to remain, something impermanent. Enjoy the process, be fully engaged in it, but don't be attached.

Old age is also marked by impermanence. But then, so is every stage of life. In old age, however, I feel it acutely. Its insistence and presence in my life are more pronounced in the changes I experience and in the lessons I learn while moving into and through those changes. Impermanence usually implies loss, and there is plenty of that as we age. My body isn't as agile, doesn't have the same level of endurance or strength. I can no longer take my body for granted as I did when I was young and I now spend more time caring for myself. I need to be mindful of how I'm treating myself; more rest, more exercise, more care in what I put into my body. The lesson I've learned is to develop a sense of self-love that is physical, that is embodied, that takes its form in how I treat myself. It's an adjustment from taking my body for granted to acknowledging the impermanence of the body and its needs. It is also a form of love; love for the self and the body I inhabit. It gives me greater appreciation for my body and its abilities. It has served me: as a child when I had boundless energy, through my teenage years when I could do physical activities for hours, as a young adult when I learned how food, exercise, rest, and stress could affect my body. But I could still ignore it, kind of. Now, as an elder I can't avoid self-care without it having consequences that I prefer not to have. I appreciate all of those stages of my physical self, many of which I've lost, but many of which I still have in modified form. I'm thankful for that, as it allows me to continue making art.

There are other forms of impermanence, such as when our friends or family members pass away. There are the sorrow and mourning that pierce relentlessly. And there is also the appreciation that they were a part of my life, part of the joy in friendship that I found, the way we so often mirrored each other, helped each other grow and process life. It also taught me to appreciate and cherish everyone I know with more depth and awareness, to acknowledge what a gift they are *now* and to be thankful for their presence in my life. It has also meant that I've let go of relationships that weren't fulfilling and nurturing as my time is precious and I want to use it wisely. A sage was asked, "What's more important, the journey or the destination?" The sage responded, "It's the company."

Another way I experience impermanence in my life is by appreciating the small, fleeting moments. Every morning I make myself a cup of tea, a light breakfast, and read the paper. Now that I'm not rushing to get out the door and off to work, I will take a few minutes to appreciate what is right in front of me; the light breeze on my skin, the smell of the flowers outside the window. One morning I sat for ten minutes and just listened to the rain, its gentle song that lasts for a time and is then gone. It made me think of Thich Nhat Hanh's take on rain. We say it's raining, but what is the "it"? Rain and raining, the same thing. It's the verb without a subject; the impermanence of the moment. It's the way most of life happens, moment to moment, only we don't really take the time to notice it. We are pushing so hard to meet the demands of life, especially the demands of middle age, which are weighty and pressing, that we don't give much time to thinking about the big picture or just being present with what is.

One morning it was the shaft of sunlight that illuminated the sprigs of wheat sheaves in a wicker vase in the window that caught my eye. They were bursting with rays of golden yellow, ripe and full of life, glowing as though emanating the light, not reflecting it. I had picked them from the side of the road where they had escaped the cultivated crop rows to grow along the edge of a Nebraska country road. I had gone there to watch the total eclipse of the sun, and seeing the glowing wheat brought me right back to that profound experience. The eclipse gave me a sense of myself being part of a larger cycle of life that transcends my small daily sphere. I felt the cosmos, the vastness of the universe, and my small part in it. The impermanence of the moon's shadow moving across the face of the sun, stopping the light and then slowly retreating was a profound awakening. The impermanence of that moment put me in touch with time, its passing, and the more vivid awareness of the moment in which I find myself. Time, in all its variability, which I sometimes experience as an arrow shooting forward in linear fashion, or as the circular time of nature and its cycles. But profound moments, like the eclipse, seem to stop time, and I enter into eternal time, the eternal now. In my older age, I have the time to muse and reflect on these things in ways I didn't have when I was pressed into the service of "getting things done."

Photography is about the small ephemeral moments. There is no later in photography; the image is now or most likely, never. If I don't take the picture in the moment I see it, later on the light won't be the same, the weather won't be the same. I won't be standing in exactly the same place. Make the photo now, in the moment, or it's gone.

Impermanence is also in my outlook of the future. I don't know what's coming. I, of course, want a vigorous and vital old age, where I am still able to do the things I enjoy, be with the people I love, have a clear mind and a functioning body. But I know that may not be what's coming. Recently one of my family members died, and we had to clear out her assisted living apartment. While taking a break in the bathroom I heard a woman's voice yelling, "Help me! Help me!" I tried to hurry and finish up to go and see if I could help. I opened the bathroom door and there was a woman in a wheelchair holding a very large baby doll blocking my exit. "Are you all right?" I asked.

"Who are you?" she angrily demanded.

"I'm a guest," I responded.

She bared her teeth, yelling, "Get out of here! Get the fuck out of here!" And she began hitting me. I was startled, shocked, and frankly, a bit scared. Not of her hitting me, but that her version of old age was so unsettling. She obviously had some form of mental health issue, Alzheimer's or dementia perhaps. That, I thought, that could be my future. And it terrified me. Because we don't know what is coming, what the impermanence of life will bring.

One of the things I have learned in life is how to hold two opposing, sometimes opposite realities at the same time. Yes, the future could be terrifying. But it could also be lovely and full of life, friends, and fun new adventures. Because impermanence isn't just loss and letting go. Impermanence is also becoming. It's something new being created, formed, brought into existence. It's the essence of art making. It changes the very nature of life. Isn't that the yin/yang of life? The impermanence of letting go and the impermanence of bringing forth are life's constant dance partners.

When there's letting go in life, it helps to have something to move toward. I recently had to move my art studio because the building was sold. I'd been there for over twenty years and had thought I would spend the rest of my days there. So when it became obvious that I would have to move, I was really heartbroken. I loved my space, loved the friends and colleagues who were part of this community. I was distraught at having to leave. But then I found a new space, close to home, so I no longer have a long commute. The space has water and a beautiful, large arched window that looks out on trees. The previous tenant had done a lot of work to fix up the space, so it was in good shape, perfect for what I would need. Knowing I had something to move toward made it a lot easier to let go. But it didn't happen on its own. I had to spend a lot of time looking for spaces. I had to trust in the flow of life and what it would bring. I know that when I make the effort, to move toward the change I want, the universe responds. It's a trust I have in the process and unfolding of life.

In the face of impermanence, my art practice is vitally important to me. It's the upside of impermanence. I'm creating, making new, feeling the flow of life energy moving through me. It's experiencing the first day of creation as a perpetual moment. It's being able to dance on that pivot of death and birth. The creativity can be whatever brings a sense of joy, of flow, of complete immersion in the doing, a letting go of the self, the "it," and instead becoming the verb. It's Rebecca, letting go of the "me" and just Rebecca-ing, like the rain. It doesn't matter what form creation takes. Perhaps it's cooking, gardening, or knitting that brings that sense of joy. Perhaps it is a traditional art form, such as writing, painting, dance, or photography. There are as many ways of creating as there are individuals. We each know when we find the experience that brings that aliveness, newness, and flow to our lives.

So old age for me is a balancing act of understanding the impermanence that pervades my life in different forms. It appears as loss and letting go, of people and things leaving and the intense emotions that brings. It is also an awareness of the richness of the fleeting moments of experiencing what is right here, right now, and how exquisite and ephemeral it all is. And I experience impermanence in the way I create, make art, and experience the joy of bringing something new into being. It's one big, complex bundle of joy, sadness, fear, yearning, celebration, excitement, and risk taking. Impermanence is the grand mystery that is life itself.

From Generation to Generation

Handing Down Art for the Ages

SUZANNE THAO

TRANSLATED BY CHUAYI (THAO) YANG

I was born in 1954 as Xyo Mim Vaj (reference to the first star next to the moon) in Phou Mou, Long Cheng, Laos. Embroidery has been a part of my life since I was born.

Grandmothers often were the first to teach the delicate art of paj ntaub: an elaborate form of sewing and the careful, intricate work of embroidery. My mother, Chia Lo, was a prolific paj ntaub maker, whose works were so sharp and precise it is hard to believe they were handmade. I was six years old when my paternal grandmother came to me and told me, "You are six years old and you are grown now. It is time for you to learn how to sew." I learned first how to cross-stitch traditional Hmong patterns, then moved on to learn the more difficult and advanced techniques of applique and reverse applique. I understood from her and the women in my home that if you can't sew, you can't marry! It was known you could not get a good husband if you couldn't display your sewing skills. Your marriage prospects were determined by your skill level.

From May 1975 to January 1976, I was in a refugee camp in Thailand. In the camp, I made friends with a girl of Yao ethnicity. Her mom gifted me with fabric and thread during this time because she saw I was very skilled and interested in it. It was hard to find embroidery thread that was colorful. I had to roam around camp, asking and collecting thread from other embroidery makers. When I finished this piece, I realized that it was only possible for me to complete it because of the generosity I found despite it being a difficult time in history and people's livelihood. Before the war, only girls did the sewing. After the war, men began to sew for money in the refugee camps in Thailand. The postwar disruption shifted Hmong paj ntaub from families making their own clothing to using Hmong paj ntaub skills and knowledge to make items for survival profit.

I got married in the refugee camp in Non Khai, Thailand, to Nhia Toua Thao in January 1976. Shortly after, we flew to and refuged in France in the same year, then in 1990 we migrated to the United States. I came with a knowledge of trauma in my body and in my memory. But I also learned how to overcome times of sorrow and find healing through the art of paj ntaub. Hmong paj ntaub is a creative process that connects me back to my place and identity in the world. Over time I put all the celebration of who Hmong people are and what they have endured in my work.

Some people look at our work and believe that it must be made by a machine, because they can't believe its intricate small stitches, from cross-stitch to appliqué on batik and reverse appliqué, can be made by hand. Now that even more machines are made to create fabric that looks like paj ntaub with similar symbols, machine-made designs are taking away from the visceral, physical connection to our art. Paj ntaub is a process that follows our journeys as Hmong women while we raise our children, overcome moments of sorrow and joy, and as we reflect and interact in spaces as grandmothers, great-grandmothers, mothers, and daughters. I want to leave this knowledge, this legacy, and this art to my Hmong community and to our sons and daughters.

For generations, it was common practice to bury a loved one's cherished embroidered pieces with them when they passed away. I don't plan to do this. I want to leave my handmade pieces for future generations to see, understand, and find the meaning and connections they seek in them for themselves.

Since 2016 I have partnered with the Hmong Museum to teach Project Paj Ntaub. It is a three-hour monthly class where participants learn and make one of the two traditional Hmong techniques: cross-stitch and reverse appliqué. I also offer one-on-one mentoring for those who want to work on personal projects.

Handmade pieces adorn Hmong skirts, hats, baby carriers, and nontraditionally decorative pieces that are for pure creative enjoyment. I observe how the color, cloth, and intricate stitching create a piece that brings joy to others and to me.

I believe there's a purpose larger than me that will direct this work and impact the livelihood of my community. My hope is that we can expand Hmong paj ntaub's reach, narrative, and legacy within and beyond the Hmong diaspora. For a long time, I didn't think my knowledge and skills of Hmong paj ntaub were valuable or important, because it wasn't producing income. Now, however, this century-old art is bringing back to life the narratives of Hmong women who have held on and fought for the legacy that lives in the art of paj ntaub and connects us to our heritage as Hmong people.

Aging has made this harder now. I have to slow down, make bigger stitches. I find smaller patterns harder to see and work with. My mind and my brain change as I age. I cannot focus as well and must accept when I am tired. When the night comes and my mind says, "You are tired now, sleep," I follow my body's order. I know this is a natural process of turning older.

What a gift paj ntaub is now. At sixty-six, I am aware that my blood pressure has slowed to a calm rate. When I feel anxiety, fear, or frustration, I pick up cross-stitch, stay present, and let the emotions subside. I am old enough and settled here. I have my home, my food. I am surrounded by my grandchildren, my children. My home is alive with colors that I created.

I only know about today! I don't know about tomorrow. So come, sit by me, and we will learn today.

For this essay, Julie Landsman recorded the three-way conversation between herself, Suzanne Thao, and her translator, her daughter, Chuayi (Thao) Yang. She put the text of the interview into essay form, received suggestions for revision from both translator and artist, and completed the final copy.

Kacee

KIM HINES

(KACEE is an older Black woman who is a writer and artist of many other things. She is about 64–68 years old. She wears a black duster over a very colorful cotton T-shirt of some sort and jeans. She wears her hair in a natural way—medium-length locks.

She sits at a small table, typing away on her laptop.

KACEE speaks directly to the audience as though they are a friend. In the silences, she types or muses about what she is writing.)

My mother passed away at 99 . . . seven months before she was to turn 100.

(silence)

I know she was pissed.

I'm sure she asked the Great Spirit up there, why bring her all the way to 99 and not let her get to 100?!

Funny, it reminds me of some of my ex-lovers who were poor "lovers" . . .

(pause)

Mom complained about her body falling apart. She said that she was expecting to find various body parts scattered throughout the house, and was concerned about tripping hazards. Wicked sense of humor she had; her mind was still sharp as a tack, though her memory was just beginning to waver some.

She talked about being in her late 60s and watching half of her friends leave before she even reached 75. By the time she was 80, she had only four friends left. Only one of them outlived her.

My father, on the other hand, passed away at 81. He knew he was leaving, he told everyone that he was leaving. He got us all ready for it about a month before he left. Oddly enough, we still weren't ready for him to leave!

My mom used to joke about his side of the family, telling you when they were going to go. It was based in some truth. I don't know how his people knew, but they knew, and some would even give you a timeline. Sometimes that timeline was a whole month, like with my dad, and sometimes it was just twenty-four hours, like with my grandmother.

(pause)

I remember, I was still in my 30s when my dad looked to me for some sort of reassurance on aging and dying. He asked me what it was like to lose so many friends to AIDS. I had stopped keeping track of the number of losses after it reached 49. My dad felt that I was too young to have lost so many friends. He mused that he was almost forty years older and had losses, but nowhere near the number that I had.

My dad asked me if I had a different take on death; did I fear it? At that time, my dad was in his 70s; no doubt he was thinking of his own mortality.

What I said to my dad was that I was going to grow older without most of my male artist friends. That was something that I feared the most, not having them there as I grew old. Death had only served as a vehicle to take my friends away from me.

(silence)

Nobody really tells you how it's going to work, this aging thing. I'm trying to divorce myself from some of the old myths about aging. I look back on my parents who had a very different take on aging . . . that's probably why they outlived so many of their friends.

(silence)

One day my mother called me, and our conversation turned to all of the kids in the family. She was blown away that she had kids who ranged in age from 78 down to 64. She asked, "Why are my kids so old?" I reminded mom she was 99 and she said, "But I don't feel 99!" And I asked her, "Well, how old do you feel?" And she said, "Today . . . I feel like I'm 52. Most days I feel like I'm in my 50s. Other times I feel like I'm in my 40s.

"Those days when I forget how old I am and I try to turn around on a dime and almost fall over, or when my arthritis is giving me problems and I can't get up from my chair even on the third try, I feel like I'm in my late 80s! Oh, my! Those 80s were a rough time for me! I'm glad I left them 80s behind!"

(chuckles)

I want to live at least as long as my mother, God willing. I've started to take a page out of her book. I've immediately stopped telling people exactly how old I am when they ask me. If they are persistent, I give them the year I was born and I let them do the math!

(pause)

I've started to identify how old I feel I am. Most days I feel like I'm in my late 30s to late 40s. That was a good time for me, and that's how I feel when I'm feeling really good.

Now it's interesting that I don't ever think about being in my 20s. I know a lot of older people who think of that period of time as their golden age. Hmmmm, not so much for me.

I remember a lot of tiredness from overworking and overpartying, and the hangovers from overdoing everything that I shouldn't have been doing! And, of course, the "Sturm und Drang" . . . the conflamma in regards to all "love" relationships. The twenties are grossly overrated!!

My late 30s and almost all of my 40s was a good time for me. And that's where I sit most days.

When my autoimmune disorder kicks up, then I feel like I'm in my 90s or at least pushing that age . . . and then I only feel that way for about forty minutes or so . . . not all at once . . . two minutes here . . . nineteen minutes there . . .

(slight pause)

But most days it's not like that at all. Most times, I sit at my dining room table . . . perched at the age of 44 . . . typing away on my laptop . . . working on a script.

(pause)

And when I am done for the day . . .

I stop to read aloud those pages to my friends who have passed over . . . hoping they can give me some good feedback.

My Re-Time-Ment

FIONA MCCRAE

It was not leaving England at age thirty-two for a job with my company's subsidiary in Boston. Not leaving Boston to run a nonprofit publishing house in the Midwest with recent financial troubles. Not being unmarried well into my thirties. Not not having kids. Not importing my mother to live near me when her memory was failing. No, it was retiring at sixty-three, after forty years of working in publishing, including twenty-eight years running the nonprofit (Graywolf Press), that caused the most people to question my plans, my life choices.

One poet told me it was world-bendingly unfathomable to him; colleagues argued that I could continue for another ten years. One agent came to my house (her only such visit) to find out for herself why I had made this decision. One donor said they felt sure I had at least one more act, if not two, in my future. And most everyone, from the accepting to the bewildered, expected me to know what I was going to *do.* Only one asked if there was a health issue.

I was unprepared both for the level of astonishment my retirement provoked and for my inability to come up with satisfying answers about it beyond limply saying I was looking forward to reading more books. Now, more than two years in, I have come to understand that my relationship to the future had changed in ways that I was unable to articulate fully at the time. It was not so much that I wanted to do different things in my future as that I felt my future might be compromised.

In 2010, my mother, aged seventy-four, newly widowed, and losing her memory, moved from England to live in a care home near me in the Twin Cities. She died of complications from Alzheimer's eight years later, after six mercifully happy years followed by thirty months in hospice when she was very diminished. Her father had died (much more quickly) of the same disease at seventy-six. When both my father's twin brother and his older sister developed forms of dementia, it brought me up short. That long stretch of unstructured free time that I had imagined opening at the end of my working life begat a cloud: I had a double chance of inheriting memory loss.

If the path to hell is paved with good intentions, my path is paved with to-be-read piles: beside the bed, on side tables, on the kitchen stool, on new and old bookshelves, on the floor, even on my iPad. Perhaps it's the same for you. The piles contain back issues of literary magazines: including the ten copies of *Granta* magazine, still unread, that I brought with me from London back in 1991. How can I throw away all those years of intending to read them?

Visions of my future involved not only my behaving differently, but time itself—or at least how I experienced time—changing. I imagined that once I was clear of the exigencies of this and that demand, time would open and slow down. That would enable future me—fueled by newfound vigor, vim, and clear purpose—to perform any number of chosen tasks. Garth Greenwell in his memoiristic novel, *Small Rain,* writes about how dehumanizing society's "instrumentalization of time" can be. I leap at that clunky word, recognizing its truth. As much as I loved my work, it also gave rise to a yearning to experience time without demands.

As the reasons to step away from the press—to create cultural, organizational, and personal change—accumulated, I realized that retirement would allow me to make up for past time given over to "required reading." More important, I could salvage stolen future time, if dementia should strike me this side of seventy-five. Future me would get to the books that I had been longing to read: some for three or four years, others for three or four decades. And this does not even count books that might be published *after* I stopped working. I needed to get on a de-instrumentalization program.

What else might that freer time offer? I told some people that the answer to what I would be doing was the very thing I was excited to find out as I lived through my one precious retirement.

But people who could not envision me ending my engagement with the literary world were right for a reason that I should have foreseen. I had always followed a personal mantra: what you do leads to what you do—your current path generates your next steps. I studied literature not as a vehicle to something else, but it did lead me to publishing. Publishing led me to a different continent. Chance conversations would lead to a new book for publication years later. Those new books in turn attracted more writers to the press. I delighted in the unpredictable ways these causal sequences unfolded.

The snag is that when you want to change what you do, the past is lacking practices to guide you forward. During those working years, I had not developed strong habits around pursuing activities for and by myself. It took retirement to show me how deep my love of collaboration, of connection with others, runs. Immediate post-retirement-me accordingly jumped into board work and freelance projects that came along. I found the work enlivening, a way to make use of familiar skills in new settings.

But the more solitary activities that I think of as being "between me and myself"—such as sorting through papers, practicing yoga and meditation, promptly reading literary magazines—have come more slowly. They were not easy before, but now I do not have the excuse of the big job pulling me away.

Over the months, though, my relationship to time has gradually evolved into something that, alongside the joys (and frustrations) of collaborating, I had an inchoate longing for. The board work does not draw me in as strongly as before. I relish the additional reading hours—for new books, old books, and still, joyfully, Graywolf books. I have learned to recognize the echoey, empty sense of time as an invitation. As I was thinking about all this, I met up with a friend with whom my husband and I have gone through many life phases. She told me she is using her retirement to shed the multitasking skills of her working self in favor of the new practice of *quieting*. Another word to borrow, this one more lyrical.

As my time quiets, I have surprised myself by starting to write. Memory loss is my theme. I am trying to capture the specific nature of this disease, its fears, its effects. I am exploring our family story, what possible future cognitive decline might mean to me, and diving into the big questions that surface when confronting the failing mind. I became interested after noticing how reluctant we are as a culture to talk frankly about dementia. It's a subject that seems both ubiquitous and buried. During the 2024 election, for example, the news cycle dodged around cognitive declines in Biden and Trump without in-depth reporting on the causes and consequences to themselves and those around them of the declines and the denials.

I mention to folk that I am writing about memory loss because it runs in my family, and they are quick to assert that I seem fine. One writer friend joked: "The fact that you are worried is some consolation." The reassurances, emphatically backed up by a neurologist, have buoyed me. But I notice how hard it is to have a truly open conversation with others about the possibility that future me might be cognitively impaired, or about how and why that possibility is frightening in the present.

Friends share their own memory slipups, laughing, eager to prove how common forgetting is. My favorite: a college friend recently commented, "Oh, I know: that thing where you forget why you walked into the room, so you have to go the previous room and work out why you went in there."

I study material on- and offline and am disappointed to see that much is by and/or addressed to caregivers for those afflicted with dementia, not to those living with it. I wonder about the differences between those who rallied around my mother when she was living with Alzheimer's and those who struggled to spend time with her. I look at how people with dementia can become invisible and contrast that with the exceptions, such as Bruce Willis's family's loving reports on his condition, which often include photographs of the actor.

My "have-read" pile of books on dementia is growing: *My Father's Brain,* by Sandeep Jauhar; *In Love,* by Amy Bloom; *Travelers to Unimaginable Lands,* by Dasha Kiper; *It Must Be a Misunderstanding,* by the Mexican poet Coral Bracho and translated by Forrest Gander. An astonishing Brit, Wendy Mitchell, has written three books that examine her experiences trying to stay one step ahead of her own Alzheimer's: they are revelation and comfort.

One of the recurring dilemmas I find myself writing through is the question of the evolving self over time. For example: to whom do we give authority over end-of-life decisions: the current self, who would not want to live beyond the loss of the mind, or to the future self, whose mind is lost and is at best content and at worst without an opinion on the matter? My mother, more than ten years before her thirty, mostly vacant, months in hospice, once told me she would "top" herself if she thought what happened to her father would happen to her. Yet, during those first six years or so years in the States, she regularly exclaimed at how happy she was.

As I draw on my forty years of working with books, my mantra "what you do leads to what you do" takes another turn, as I realize that what you publish can influence what you write. I had wondered about calling the manuscript *Memory Tests,* then I realized that sounds too like the title whose structure is often in mind: *The Empathy Exams,* by Leslie Jamison. I think about Ésme Weijun Wang's book about living with schizophrenia—like dementia, a disease that others frame as robbing one of the self. A subtle Dutch novel I worked on years ago when I was a junior editor at Faber and

Faber in London has long resonated with me. J. Bernlef's *Out of Mind* is narrated by a man losing his memory. (I was so proud when I helped translate the title: a phrase whose second meaning could suggest the theme.) I pose direct questions on the page, not my favorite literary device, but I am reassured when I remember Sven Birkerts, an author who wields wily rhetorical questions in service of his gorgeous prose. When I think about all the phrases we have for dementia (dotty, away with the fairies, mad as a hatter), I recall Graywolf poet Nick Flynn's long list of terms for drunk that appears in *Another Bullshit Night in Suck City.* As I try to dig into gnarly questions, I remember Eula Biss's *On Immunity,* how she took her queries to medical experts, and how all of us at Graywolf loved to see her think through a question on the page.

Although I am a writer in the sense that I now spend time writing, I don't consider myself a *writer*-writer. I have not dedicated my life to the act of it; I am only tentatively starting out. But I love this chance to explore the art. I experience for myself observations that authors shared with me about their process over the years: "I am writing the book I want to read that does not seem to exist yet"; "I write to understand"; "I don't know in advance what I will write but I discover in the writing the direction the piece wants me to go in"; "I use writing to interrogate my assumptions." I remember how I always felt accused, shallow, in the light of Socrates's quote about writing: "The unexamined life is not worth living."

I never imagined I would be this side of the writer–editor pencil. When the pencil was in my hand, I thought a piece of writing edited itself: I expected the authors had already intuited what sentences I would push back on. But with my own piece, I know I would never have seen at least half the comments I got back from a magazine editor, who was spot-on about places that could be cut. When she kept me waiting for months, I could not help identifying with the pressure I knew she was under from other submissions. Please, please don't feel guilty, I wanted to reassure her.

I start to covet time as an opportunity to write as well as read. Yet I distract myself haplessly and foolishly. There is always news to follow about the horrors of war, the latest political failure, the ravages of climate change, the recently deceased celebrity whose clips I feel compelled to watch on YouTube. Who has time for one person's thoughts about dementia?

I wonder if I will ever catch up with the future me who moves serenely through her list of intentions? After an hour or so of writing, she moves closer, and I feel better in mind and body, as after a swim or a yoga class. I can almost believe that writing is good for my health. Though nothing can take away whatever decline and demise time has in store for me, writing has helped me slow down time, which in turn keeps the fears about diminished me at bay.

I feel a certain urgency to the work, as I argue to myself that an unexamined disease is not worth having. And writing is leading to more writing. The first, thousand-word piece eventually grew into a longer essay. Then additional pieces followed and now a book-length manuscript is forming. Writing does not even seem solitary anymore. I smile when I recognize that the first piece I wrote was in response to two external requests. One from the magazine editor, the other from a creativity group I wandered into during my first months of retirement. My collaborative self enjoys sharing the work and receiving feedback.

Writing about memory led me to time. Time is my subject, my desire, my enabler, my threat, my solace. I circle it as I spend my retirement (my re-time-ment). I have more of it and recognize more keenly its fleetness. I learn to savor the increment, especially the de-instrumentalized increment, and try to trust my own advice: a slice of time well spent will lead to another slice of time well spent. I quiet. I write.

Three Poems

JOYCE SUTPHEN

At the Clinic

I present myself at the desk,
my driver's license and insurance card
in hand, my disease carefully locked
inside the body they will measure
and weigh when I am called.

In the waiting room I wait, I get up
and I sit down. I stand in front of
a photograph I've come to love
after many months here—
I've gotten to know it; I'm there
with the barn cats and horses.

When my name is called, I hesitate,
wanting, for a moment, not to be me,
not to have to recite (again) the litany of
what I know they know—
as well as I do—doesn't have a cure.

But I have come, as one must do, and I
will list my medications and explain how

I am adjusting to the waning days
and the long nights, when (I do
not say how often) I cannot sleep.

I tell the doctor, "I lack ambition."
He says my goal must be
to get it back again.

The Short Bio

For days I couldn't get past the short bio—
the little paragraph that could sum up

my life, just-like-that: born, married, children.
Divorced, retired, and soon (no doubt) deceased.

There seemed little else worth writing about.
All of the things I had been about

to remember were abandoned in favor
of the broad stroke—the pictogram of my life.

Behold a tree and the sun caught in it.
See the pipe and the sign under it which reads:

"This is not a pipe," in French. I wanted
to take snapshots of myself so that

I would remember the moments when I least
expected to see myself again; I wanted

to slip back into the body that never
suspected how much it was like a cloud.

Burial Notes

No lipstick, no fingernail polish.
My rings? Ok, but no necklace.

That black top I always wore,
and blue jeans—the old ones. No belt.

A book of poetry—the one
on the bedside table—

and a Moleskine and a pen.
I know, I know . . .

indulge me, ok? And if you're feeling
generous: some seashells,

flat black stones
from Lake Superior,

and the photo that is behind
the one of you on the dresser.

What Time May Not Heal

DIANE WILSON

When I first met my husband, Jim Denomie, at a Solstice party twenty-nine years ago, I heard a distinct inner voice telling me, "You've got time." This voice has guided me over the years, once even telling me to take out a loan to finish my first book. But on that particular night, those words signaled that this was a significant encounter, that I would have time to develop whatever relationship was to come next. He called three days later and we were together from then on, a relationship that lasted twenty-seven years until his death in 2022.

When we first met, I was a single mother with a dream of becoming a writer, and Jim was newly sober and a recent graduate from art school. Shortly after we married in 2002, we stumbled onto our dream home—a small cabin on ten acres with a tamarack bog—and spent a year building studios for each of us. I wrote early in the morning before sunrise, listening to the birds greet the day, surrounded by the deep quiet of farm fields and woods. The lack of visible neighbors felt like balm, a solitude that was interrupted only by an occasional browsing deer. Jim's studio above the garage fired up in the evening with loud, foot-tapping music that fueled the riot of color on his canvases. Twenty years rolled by, enough to confirm my belief in the endless generosity of time. Jim grew into an internationally known artist, and I published five books and multiple essays. Together, we built a stable, sober, creative life. Our shared family legacies of Native boarding schools and alcoholism had been transformed.

Where I made a mistake early on was in thinking that the time we had been given was limitless. With all the unreal optimism of youth (the forties seem young to me now), I still believed that we were somehow immortal, that illness and accidents and untimely death happened to other people. Even as his pillbox grew larger over the years and he dealt with prostate cancer, I was convinced that we would vanquish every health challenge and live to old age.

When the pandemic forced Jim to retire from his day job as a drywall taper, he was thrilled to focus completely on his art. Our retirement plan was simple: social security would cover our mortgage, allowing us to work full-time as artist and writer. When I retired from nonprofit work in September 2021, we made plans for a road trip the following April to visit friends and family in Texas and New Orleans. In the meantime, he was focused on creating work for the most significant show of his career that would open at the Minneapolis Institute of Art. I was busy promoting my new novel. Endless, joyful time.

On April 10, 2022, instead of packing for our road trip, I was hosting a memorial for a community of friends and family and artists who were devastated by my husband's unexpected death from cancer. The grief of our community was expressed through boundless generosity, as cards, flowers, gifts of food, and art flooded our home in those early weeks. Many, many people told me how much they loved him, what a great man he was. All true. My family and friends held me up, stayed with me, cooked endless meals, hovered nearby. But inevitably, the time came when the door closed behind the last houseguest, and I was alone. Out of time. Surrounded, immersed, smothered in a new, breathless silence.

When asked if I would write an essay for this anthology, I agreed, thinking I could come up with something wise and deep, an elder ruminating on life and loss. Instead, the more I thought about what

I would write, the more I realized that I was mostly pissed off. I felt betrayed by time, by the promise of a life I had naively believed would last. Had I known how fragile our lives truly are, how easily we can be upended by a rogue cell, by the lingering damage of early trauma, I might have done something differently with the hope it would give us more time. There would never be enough, I know that now, but still I wish. In the numb shock that followed loss, I stopped writing, gardening, and cooking. I no longer knew who I was. How could I possibly write an essay when all I had to share was a simmering angry depressed anxiety. Every day I did my best to practice deep gratitude for our many years together, for the life we created, for the joyful memories I hold. It's not enough.

I also tried reading books and articles on grief, how to get on with life after a devastating loss. I talked with a counselor at the hospice service who agreed with me that I would not be a good fit for a grief group. I've exhausted family and friends with my sadness, and I've exhausted myself with travel to escape being home alone. I know that time heals grief. But does it also heal rage?

Anger can be a mask for unexpressed grief, as sometimes it's easier to be angry than it is to do the deep hard work of grieving. But there is another way to think about anger and rage. These emotions can also emerge as a response to injustice, especially ongoing systemic violence toward Indigenous men, women, and children. Generations have experienced assimilation policies intended to dispossess Native people from their homelands, cultures, and spirituality, often by targeting children. Grief that is fueled by oppression can spark into rage capable of burning down cities. When this ongoing cultural violence claims the life of a loved one, then we can claim our anger as righteous.

As generations of Native men have experienced wars and removals and the constant reminder that they were unable to protect their families, the weight of that history now means that they have the lowest life expectancy of any racial or ethnic group, according to the National Indian Council on Aging. Jim understood firsthand the toll that early trauma has on a body. When we first met, he was slowly rebuilding his life after two decades of alcoholism. He grew up in a family that knew poverty, addiction, and removal from the reservation as part of the federal relocation program. His grandparents went to boarding school, the assimilation plan that destroyed the well-being of generations of Native families. Jim, and so many others, used alcohol as a way to mask the pain and trauma that has been the experience of countless Native children. The miracle is that he found his way to sobriety, to art school, and that he never lost his kind, gentle, loving spirit.

When Native children grow up with hunger, lack of access to health care, when they learn early to drink and smoke and take drugs to dull the heartbreak they've both inherited and experience daily, when they battle depression and anxiety, then that legacy lives on in their damaged livers, in their susceptibility to diabetes and high blood pressure, to the cancer that rises too young. Then we lose men like Jim, whose brilliant talent was at its peak, whose life was a role model for so many artists, who was beloved by his family and his community. Who do I hold accountable for this unspeakable loss? Where do I channel my anger so that no more children are sacrificed to the racism that is built into this country's foundation? How do I heal a grief that is rooted in genocide? Tell me how time will heal this wound.

A Native scholar, Rachel Flowers, has written, "You will never have my forgiveness as long as land dispossession, domination, and violence are present in the lives of Indigenous peoples." When I was younger, I might have agreed with her. But then I interviewed elders for a book, *Beloved Child,* to understand how we transform the rage that burns alongside this history into a better way of life for our children. That's when I started to see how anger, like fire, can be life-giving and energizing, as well as destructive, especially to the person carrying it. Forgiveness allows us to let go of its caustic force but does not erase the injustice that needs to be remediated. Forgiveness protects our hearts so that we can tend to the most important work of all—reclaiming that which was taken away, harmed, shamed, murdered, and destroyed—so that our children and grandchildren grow up surrounded by love and knowing their culture, history and identity.

Despite all of the hard challenges in Jim's life, he knew that his family loved him. In turn, he loved his children and worked to become the best father and grandfather he could be. He still carried anger toward the ongoing racist treatment of Native people but he expressed it through his art, using relentless, humorous, pointed references to current and historical events and leaders. Through his imagination and his brilliant use of color, he transformed his anger into a powerful story of reclamation and resilience that will continue on long into the future.

Two years after Jim's death, I am still learning how to carry my anger and grief from the plants and animals who share our land. In the early months of Jim's absence, I developed a fear of the dark, of its heavy silence, newly aware that my home was isolated from people. As dusk settled each night into long shadows, I began sitting outside on my front porch with my dog, crazy Annie, leaning against my shoulder. While she sniffed the air, I gazed at the sky and watched for shooting stars. By listening deeply, I could hear the rustle of a night-dwelling animal moving in the brush, or the call of the barred owl, who-cooks-for-you, from a distant tree. Some nights, the wind would rustle the leaves on the birch trees that surround my yard. I might see the dim flutter of a bat's wings overhead. By allowing the night to enfold me, to reveal its true nature, its mystery and beauty, I could set down my fear and my grief and find peace. If I woke at 3 a.m., that loneliest of hours, I remembered the stars.

Some days I head out into the fields, wearing my army green

vest with many pockets, and observe who lives here and why. What plants offer food, a place to nurture growing babies? Snapping turtles lay their eggs on the side of my gravel driveway, while sandhill cranes shake a tail feather as they dance for their mates in my neighbor's field. Learning about this land has helped me know this place as my home once again, a feeling I lost when Jim died. I have a commitment now to slow time, to incremental healing, knowing that the sight of young rabbits playing is what I need most. They remind me daily that I'm never alone, that we are all connected through place, by sharing this land. This is the work that is redefining my writing and, ultimately, my life.

In the time that is left to me on this earth, I hope to grow into this new life and transform my experience into writing that holds space for what angers me as well as for love and beauty that can be shared with the world.

The Circumference of My Life

JULIE LANDSMAN

One prose poem, two in verse, allow me to discover and acknowledge what being eighty means. Looking at my life as a writer and painter, from the perspective of a short remaining lifespan, I see new angles, new truths about love, family, history.

Writing at each stage of my life has always allowed me to discover my own mind. Letting the pen go, the images come, then revisiting a chapter, a landscape has allowed me to measure the circumference of my life. I remember whole scenes: who I was at a certain time, who I am now, where I came from to get here. I am grateful to writing and, later in life, to painting to teach me what *perspective* means: seeing from a new angle of years.

The poem/letter below was written to my father while I was spending days in Hanoi. He had died ten years before. It took me time to be able to write it. I was alive when a national movement called for US troops to be brought out of Vietnam. I lost friends to the war and to prison then.

Only after he was gone did I understand the depth of my separation from my father during those years.

Dear Father,

I am here in Hanoi and I want to say you must arrive in this country with a heart willing to break: for the torn earth, the blue building leaning on the yellow one, the old woman under the arc of the thick branch across her back. I don't know what you would make of my sorrow here.

Jazz at night and I feel you, ten years after we sent you into earth, daffodils in April snow. In this Asian land that split us apart, I listen to Sinatra songs, a man plays alto on a dented sax. Oh, hip father in the basement on insomniac nights, your trumpet underneath my sleep, I want to show you the way the long haired man in the yellow shirt gets the saxophone phrasing just right, and how too, after jazz and dinner on a veranda in moonlight, a twisted girl with harelip and splayed walk chased us into the street, begging.

An old woman with blackened teeth spit into the pond at the Temple of Literature, as we walked the red and black lacquered rooms, Buddha resting on fat thighs in incense.

And still the music, "My Way" or "Laura," your hand rests on my shoulder: here in a city of roosters perching under lamp posts, women assembling the best green fruit.

A red bridge curves over Lake Han, mist hovers, and your favorite tree, the willow, enters my lens.

Once you planted roses, your back bent in the July sun of Connecticut as I rode horses in the fields nearby.

Now my husband, Maury, and I walk among colors dumbstruck by what was done here.

In Hanoi, the women collect below their slant of rooms and, perhaps, gossip.

On the corner, near the Hang Guy silk road, there is a café.

An angry woman sits on the corner yelling.

A man in a black shirt darts away when Maury gets out his camera while teen girls giggle, pose over curves of bananas, pyramids of lemons.

His lens captures them in light, shade; careful of intrusion. We are standing in the absence of old men, the space left empty.

Another night and jazz in the lobby of the Hanoi Hilton Opera Hotel.

A young man plays an ancient saxophone, bends Sinatra as smooth as any you ever loved.

"One for the Road"; whisper of sorrow here in the monsoon city.

On the way to the airport we drive in and out of a million scooters.

Yellow shirts, green scarves, appear and disappear beside us, glass thick between our lives.

In the rice paddies, black shirts, cylindrical hats, call back scenes from war clips.

Try and imagine the size of American GIs in such a small boned place.

Just this: these women, men, children clutched on the back of vespas, their presence, their sorrow, came between us.

I want you alive to tell you: unbearable juxtapositions: the entrance of trumpet and piano, the old grandmother who lived through white flare of bomb light on her balcony.

What I want to say is I loved you all the years we did not speak.

Only here do I know this. And too, from years between us, can I see my young and righteous self with unflinching love.

In art class, I am able to create in a visceral way what was happening far from where I lived.

This after seeing a *New York Times* photograph of flooding in Cambodia:

I believe

When I draw the girl standing in the doorway clutching
the sill with her toes to keep away from the flood waters
running through her street
When I feel my pencil curving around her body, her
right hand clutching a few pieces of fruit and some rolls
in a plastic bag
When I sketch her muscular legs, beautiful as a ballerina
reaching for light
I believe I am finding comfort

When I draw the soldier, his wife and baby, stretched out on
the ground, curled up in each other's arms,
When I work and work on the downturn of his mouth
When I erase and redraw the trust of the baby's sleep-
ing face
I believe a burden is lifted

When I take a pen for the fine lines in the drape of the
Afghan woman's burqa
When I find her face somewhere, faint behind the scrim and
place her eyes there
When I try, with ink only, to capture the blue, the yellow, the
emerald of her friends' draping
I believe melancholy lightens.

Some comfort in the feel of pencil encircling each of them:

yet, not for those I draw, those caught in the still life of
each photo;
not for them the relief, the end to flood or loss or fear.
Rather for me, the one who sees and draws
because she finds the world unbearable.

A final realization that comes to me in many assorted guises is that I may be the one of the two of this long marriage left alone at the end of my life. I wrote the following poem wrestling with this thought, with Maury's ritual upbringing and my lost connection to the church where I was raised.

Again, it is writing that allows this view from the angle of an aging married woman the chance to recognize what fear, what grief is here in me, now. We are taught to consider perspective when we draw the angle of one building next to another: how distance is revealed by the placement of a tree out in a field, a house even further out, a bird circling the scene. Aging has brought perspective, seeing things close-up, feeling time shorten possibilities.

Stranded in the middle of Hebrew

For Maury

Shabat services. You dipped and rocked your body.
I watched this you I never knew,
listened to words I never said, songs I never sung.
Ritual brought no comfort,
Left me vigilant: when to stand, when to sit,
use the prayer book from back to front.

Now you are in Morocco.
You, the truest atheist I have known,
visit synagogues, eat Friday Sabbath dinners
with families in Casablanca, Marrakech.

Our disconnect is not just distance
but a separation of childhoods: the hymns
in daily chapel at St. Margaret's,
Christmas eve when ten-year-old Cindy Childs
sang the purist notes to "Oh Holy Night" I have ever heard.

Your severe uncles stood
at each corner of the Chuppa for our wedding.
In Uncle Ott's house were separate dishes
for Passover, long ceremony around the table,
children restless for matzo ball soup
                                        that would signal the meal
                                        would begin.

Without you here, I walk the dog, re-create our evenings,
make dinner for one, watch the news.

I am un-moored, imagine
you will return to ask me to go to Shul with you
each Friday, where I will feel abandoned
                              even as my shoulder touches yours.

Home is not where we come from
but rather home is where we are at ease.

I am at ease when you are here, the you
Who defied your mother, your father, to marry me.
I am at ease when you are nearby, so I do not have to wonder
how safe the bus rides into the Atlas Mountains,
or breakdowns out on the Sahara.

Has it come to be that we have made a home
Of our bodies, awkward in bed as we age,
            adjusting to fragility, rigidity of neck or knee?
Has it come to be that you are home to me?

Right here in these rooms could be where you leave me,
not for Shul, or the seders, or the group where you
study Torah;

not for the kugel that tastes like your Aunt Flo's, or for
the arguments
with Uncle Morty over Israel and Palestine.

Here where death bides its time.

The United Church of Christ holds no comfort for me.
I was raised in a family that loved with conditions.
Yet I was not unloved.
It was simply that I
never felt at home
in those early rooms where I grew.
This space, this kitchen, this small deck with plants in spring,
Could be where I lose you in the end.

Now, I understand nights of sitting Shiva.
Hold close what I may need
from your ancestors.
Rituals I can inhabit when my time of grief comes.

Female Self-Portraiture and Me

SHARI ALBERS

Inner dialog and self-expression are core components of any self-portrait. An image may document a specific moment or event in the artist's life or may exhibit drama, fantasy, or comedy. A pose may be manipulated, costumes worn, or props added to boast accomplishment or societal position, or to make a political statement. Historically, artists sometimes portrayed themselves at work to attract prospective clients. And, of course, most self-portraits we are familiar with were made by men.

Women artists had been creating art for a thousand years and more. Self-portraits by women were not uncommon. Until the 1970s, when women demanded exposure to female art history, few had known of medieval nun illuminators Claricia, Diemoth, and Guda, who inserted images of themselves in their elaborate manuscript initials. *On Famous Women,* an illustrated book published in 1402, features Iaia of Cyzicus (now called Marcia), seated and holding a hand mirror while painting her own portrait.

The Renaissance era brought about artistic realism and emotive characters, as well as the development of better mirrors. Artemisia Gentileschi (1593–1656), Judith Jans Leyster (1609–1660), Giovanna Fratellini (1666–1731), and Elisabeth Vigée-Lebrun (1755–1842) painted themselves at their easels. Holding the tools of their trade, these women artists look directly at the spectator and proclaim their artistic skills with full self-confidence.

Mexican artist Frida Kahlo (1907–1954), her body shattered by childhood polio and a horrific bus accident, painted fifty-five vibrant self-portraits depicting her pain, anguish, and surrealistic imagination. Portraitist Alice Neel (1900–1984) illustrated herself numerous times before painting her first nude self-portrait at age eighty. Faith Ringgold (1930–2024) created self-portraits in paint, in textiles as "story quilts," and as illustrated children's picture books. Since the 1970s feminist movement, women artists have transformed contemporary art. Photographer Cindy Sherman (b. 1954) inserts her own face and body into various imagined characters that challenge masculinity, femininity, and pop culture. Kiki Smith (b. 1954), a multidisciplinary artist who focuses on the female figure and nature, has drawn herself grieving for her dying cat and has projected herself as an old woman.

I was sixty-two when my husband's sudden death catapulted me into self-portraiture. The work started as a memoir detailing many aspects of a widow's grief. Then, an intense studio course switched my point of view from written word to visual. Self-portraiture was not new to me. Twenty-some journals encase intimate self-renderings and words that have been key to understanding and valuing my physical being. More than thirteen years later, whether gazing in a mirror or at a staged cell phone selfie, I encounter a droopier, thicker, and more textured me.

My age sixty-eight version dominated three acrylic paintings I created during June 2018. A devious me battles my dead husband's 113 rose bushes. A conflicted me hugs the house we spent our entire marriage renovating. A nearly insane me poses with thirty-one dead mice. A first art exhibit and the resulting conversations with onlookers confirmed my work touched people. Some widows recognized themselves. Some were relieved to find odd or frantic situations common. Artist and program mentor Elizabeth Erickson hailed the sad humor and captioned visuals of the series as "never been done before." Exuberant reactions and shared tears prompted me to continue painting grief images for another four years.

A distressed me addresses insurance woes. A hallucinating me sees my dead husband's face in a ceiling fan. An angry me takes a chainsaw to his beloved mulberry tree. An ethereal me sees my husband reincarnated as a turtle. At some point in the process, I separated from the agony that originally drove my work. When its first solo exhibition opened in 2022, *The Widow Series* had grown to seventeen self-portrait paintings. Today, there are eighteen.

Birthed from the written word, my drawings of noted objects and whimsical facial expressions morphed into self-portrait compositions. Then, the self-portraits demanded words. My creative cycle spun full circle, from language, to image, to full compositions blending both word and image to tell a story of one widow's devastation, anxiety, and resilience.

Frida Kahlo revealed her damaged body and broken heart. Alice Neel defiantly exposed her eighty-year-old vulnerable body. Kiki Smith dared to age into her imagined future for all to see. Upon the strength of these women artists and others, I found the courage to unveil my own struggles and triumphs as I stumbled through the aftermath of loss.

(The Loop) Umbria Minnesota (The Spiral)

JoANN VERBURG

Rome Airport:

Well, it's different but it's still Italy.

Umbria

Spoleto morning
Sometimes I ask myself,
why am I here?
It's for reasons I can't answer.
I need to remember that.

On The Loop, the senses:
    The burnt grass smell,
The stars,
    The wind,
The cicadas,
    What's the other one? The taste of garlic . . .

[oh] . . . and WONDER.

Passing through Piazza Campello:
He will sit today here on the bench
in the shade of umbrella pines and the great Cedar of Lebanon,
With his mouth open.
His clothes are loose
like pajamas.
Later, he will tilt his head.
He looks at everything,
engages with no bird or man
or the four black cats
who are fed under the edge of a car.
They know where to find food. It's the kindness of strangers
 that keeps
them here in Piazza Campello. For water, they go to the fountain,
Open their mouths,
Tilt their heads.

11 July, 11 pm, 2020
Jimmy: well, it's a little harder being nice than being cranky,
but not much.

Embrace discombobulation!

On The Loop last night

Repositioning
Repositioning
so that exactly
centrally
behind the cross of lights on Monteluco,
Rose the moon.

Minnesota
Spiral

April 5

Me, while speaking to Jim, being "interrupted"
by an unmasked jogger slowly coming toward us,
then a masked jogger
slowly running past us; and losing my train of thought.

When everything drains down to nothing, one seems like
something.

Mississippi River
It's actually not a beautiful star.
It's an airplane.
Do you still like it?

At the foot of the bridge
As we walked by, an old man with a cigarette,
                    seated on a rock:
                          "Hey! Hah, thank you for not running!"

Minneapolis, jet-lagged morning
Look! There's only one
cloud in the sky,
and the moon
found it.

Umbria, The Loop

2018-12-1
Sex as though there's sex,
a bath as though there's water in the tub,
Your grief, as though I'm with you,
now, as though there is a future.
That's today. That's how it is going.

On The Loop
Despite earthquakes,
people are getting married,
visiting Spoleto as we also did
on our honeymoon. Look
at the blonde in white: White
jacket, White blouse, White silk
trousers, leaning on his arm,
Tippy in her White heels, talking too loud, slurring the word:
"Polenza!"

American tourist outside a caffè:
I gotta go to Perugia and buy some shirts.
I only brought uno.

5-13-19 on The Loop
The last holdouts are giving
In
To
Spring

Spiral

From a bridge over the Mississippi River
If you're an eagle
or a person,
start like him:
sit on a pier or a jetty.
Looking this way, toward the falls,
and that way toward the city.

11-1-17 Minneapolis café
Did she give it to you by ESP? (I asked about my order.)

No, she verbaled it.

Umbria

7-20-2018
A very old man stops ahead of me on The Loop. He is dressed in tan clothes the right length but they are too wide for him: Ma-na-gia! he cries, MAH-NAAHHJ' JJJAH! looking down. Now his back is straightening, now after a pause, he is bending again, now moving his cane forward. I hear it tapping the street. Clack . . . (slowly) clack . . . (slowly) clack . . . His left hand curls to the center of his back, palm out toward me, where it stays. Clack . . . clack . . . clack . . . clack . . .

6-16-19
"Paralyzing disproportions."
Arshile Gorky

10-24-21
Mostly I'm just tired, I say to Jim.
I haven't slept more than about six hours the last four nights.
To myself:

WHY AM I DOING THIS?

Spiral, Minneapolis

USA
Getting off the phone with Kristine:
I love hearing your voice.
It reminds me of you.

On the Stone Arch Bridge

Where's the moon?
. . . It's with the swallows.

Sunrise 4-28-19

The sun is rising, and I must avert
my eyes, but I don't. I can't help
myself. What will I do with
this blessing
—a new day—
a day no one ever has lived?

Will I, like yesterday—a day past—regrettable—
Spend it in darkness?

Walking around Lake Nokomis

". . . my grandmother: sometimes I'm not sure she knows that
I'm an adult yet . . . or whatever."

12-06-20?

Like my Venice Shade Walk, I find myself trying to concoct
a successful complicated plan that will allow me to do
something simple.

"Stuck is not stuck."

Mike Tucker

The Loop, Italy

9-9-19 Monteluco di Spoleto

A gray frizzy-haired gal
tucked in

at the edge of the forest.
Crouched down.
Blooming. Colors. Goldenrod. Thistles.
Late summer
weeds.
As we pass, her back to us—
doing email.

6-16-19
Crossing a bridge
in Venice,
Older white man in shorts to
younger white man in shorts:
. . . Well, that's how you hedge!
        and you can ALSO short futures . . .

The Spiral, Minnesota

13 September 2020
me: You looked at me like I was speaking a foreign language.
you: You were . . .
The language of the hearing.

8-24-17
Jo to Jim:
THIS IS INTERESTING!
. . . Well,
kind of interesting . . .

not at all interesting.

Loop, Umbria

3-8-21
The solution to everything is to let go of the problem.

3-24-21
"Only one magnificence at a time."
Jim

Minnesota, The Spiral

March 27
It's not a photo; it's a tree.

March 25, 2021
On Palm Springs domestic architecture:
Some of it is theatrical and some of it is ostentatious,
and each one provides
cover for the other.

02-20-2023
From this distance
I can't tell if it's a drone or
—actually there are
two—but are they military helicopters, or floating
immobile blackbirds?

April 10, 2021
Ah, sunglasses.
A wasted wink!

1-14-21
Augmented reality.
Me: It's not that interesting.
Jim: No. It just reminds you how much is missing.

Umbria, The Loop

9-22-2021
Walking past the sites of many failed photos, yet it does not seem like a failure.

8-10-21
"If you want me, I'll be somewhere between where we were and here."
Sophia Janowitz

10-1-2021
Jimmy: Well . . . I can't not write about the mourning doves . . .

Minnesota, The Spiral

Sidewalk, 8-29-23
Three men (strangers):
"It's not as . . ."
"What if . . ."
"If we could . . ."

9-17-23
Eagle
and seagull.
But that doesn't make it poetry.

Sun up before me this morning.
It couldn't wait.

The Loop, Umbria

27 January 2022
I love it,
he said. You're so lost in the moment.

. . . No, I'm not lost,
I said, I'm found in the moment.

End of April or early May, 2024
Jimmy: It's like a dream. You're dreaming; your dream is in
another world, and you wake
up, and this is it.

10-7-23
Jim: . . . but I didn't know what it all means.
Jo: What it all means is that it's time for us to go outside and
walk down the hill and get a caffè.

Minnesota

9 August 2024
A revelation,
after I admitted my crabbiness:
The show I've been working on for years now
is my statement of healing.
It's not healing itself,
but the aftermath
of change,
of letting go,

of being in darkness without denial,
light without victory.

Jimmy 9-27-24
My hearing aids say to me first thing in the morning
first this one
then that one
"Normal."

. . . Do you know who you're talking to?

5-15-24
"I rely on May."
Michael Dennis Browne

The Loop

9-20-21
Jo: I think what we're here for is not what we thought we
were here for.

Jim: Well,
That happens . . .

This writing was made on Verburg's cell phone while taking walks in one of two countries where she currently lives with her husband, poet Jim Moore. In the United States, she walks along the Mississippi River, often on a path that spirals up a small man-made hill. She also stops to jot something down in Umbria, Italy, often on a pedestrian road that loops around the ancient castle of Spoleto.

Delicious Time 101

MIEKO YAMAZAKI

"The secret of life / is enjoying the passage of time." My favorite song, "Secret O' Life," written by James Taylor, starts with this. At the age of seventy, I find it resonates in me often.

Throughout decades as an artist, there have been many problems and challenges I have had to face. For example, right after I graduated from Minneapolis College of Art and Design, my right shoulder did not move at all because of excessive use I made of it for painting, drawing, etc. As a result, I ended up in a surgery and a long rehabilitation period. For a few years I could not create any art at all. I was unable to use the traditional method of painting on a canvas with an easel as that would put more stress on my damaged shoulder.

I needed to find a new painting method to ease shoulder pain. It took years with many trials and failures. But I finally found a method using chemical reactions with oil paints and mediums on a board because chemical reactions would not be clear on a canvas. And 90 percent of its process would be done on a flat table that does not tax my shoulder much. Yet it has been always a "work in progress," since no one used the method before and chemical reactions are different color by color. When each problem/challenge happens, I struggle and try, try, try . . . again, again, and again. Whatever the issue (technical, compositional, aesthetic . . .) is, the solution to it can be elusive.

It is true those problems made me as I am now: I had to accumulate techniques and knowledge through problem solving. Yet, ultimately, the best thing I learned was that problems could not be solved overnight: they can take a long time, even years of trials and failures. Even now, practices, learning techniques, research, and conversations with other artists may or may not help solve what I want to do. There are always unsolved mysteries. After decades of challenging these obstacles, I finally understand that art making has never been about techniques or knowledge. Nor has it been about getting approval or a reputation from others. For me it turned out to have been a time to challenge myself: exploring uncharted fields with boldness, courage, and long-lasting persistence. And, some days, if I am very lucky, something breathtaking to me will appear as part of my creation.

There is a parable of a Chinese painting master. His apprentice asked him what art was. After contemplating awhile, the master answered, "It is infallible techniques and if you are fortunate, you might see art there."

Sometimes there is something wonderful and inexplicable that appears in art that can move us deeply. We can't explain it with techniques and logic; it is an element that appeals to our mind directly without description or clever ideas. Often, we have a similar experience in nature. Looking at a magnificent sky, listening to sound of a stream, touching tree trunks. . . . , we feel pure joy. We are refreshed. These sights and sounds and light speak to our minds directly without any words or skills. All artists hope to have such a reaction from viewers of their work. We aim for it each time we create art. We learn and work hard to get it on our painting, sculpture, dance, our song. . . . And to be honest we know it won't often happen.

When everything does come together, it is a special time for an artist. Her creation goes smoothly as she envisioned, and she sees something she has never done, and more. I call it "delicious time." It is an experience that not many people get to have in their various professional fields. What a beautiful time it is! Almost euphoric. And when it happens for me, I wish to be there forever. But it is not like that all the time. In fact, most of the time a painting can end up with the artist feeling disappointed. But even so, we still get to have precious time exploring, invigorating, hoping for that "delicious moment." And finally when it does happen—when we feel we have created what we wanted on the board or canvas, the paper, in clay, print, or photograph—it is the finest kind of a day and we let ourselves enjoy it.

As I age, my paintings are changing because I am changing. They may not have the bouncing energy I used to have, but there are more times for me now, of curiosity, appreciation for my surroundings, calmness, and most of all, enjoyment!

Time I can focus and concentrate is getting shorter now than when I was younger. My mentor, John Slorp, used to say, "When I get older, I may become unable to communicate with you. But if you'd see me doodling on a paper with crayons, that means I am enjoying it." During his final years Henri Matisse could not paint or sculpt due to his illness, so he created collages. A friend of mine, a watercolorist, had difficulty retaining words as she aged. But she decorated her sink, doorknob, kitchen table with leaves, twigs, and stones that she picked up. Artists are fortunate people because we know how to enjoy our lives with art making, no matter our age or physical ability.

The song at the beginning of this writing ends with, "It's just a lovely ride."

At the end of my life, I might be impaired physically or mentally and unable to continue painting. Who knows! But if I have moments as I grow old, aware that art making has made my life a lovely ride, I will be content with what I have accomplished.

We will see . . .

Nose to Nose

Sally and Hazel (1960 to 2013)

HAZEL BELVO

We were both twenty-five. We were both wearing black cocktail dresses. High heels. Long hair. We met at a party in New York City at Ruth Speaker's loft. And we stood nose to nose as Sally always said. Year after year. Born the same year. A city girl and a country girl. We both grew up in a family of secrets. We looked alike. We were artists.

We were both in love! Sally with a British jazz piano player and I with an Ojibwe abstract painter! Then we were both pregnant. Pushing our baby carriages, we marched for world peace with one hundred mothers from the United Nations Building to First Street. We listened to Miles Davis. Thelonious Monk. George Coleman. Aretha Franklin. I painted Sally.

Sally said she was left on a doorstep; that when her German mother was sixteen she came to this country on a ship, alone, worked as a housemaid, met a seaman, had two children, and became a young widow. About six years later, a couple knocked on her door and asked her to take care of their baby until they came back. They never came back. Sally was that baby. She was always looking for them, this couple, always trying to solve the mystery, and longing to know why she was abandoned. We were so alike that one day she said, "Hazel, where was your father in November 1933?" We both laughed but wondered: Sister artists by choice?

When my mother was sixteen, she was allowed by her very restrictive father to go to a summer church camp where she met a lifeguard seven years her senior. A straight A student who had never missed a day of school, a born scientist who intended to be a doctor, she came back to her farm home pregnant. When my father returned from naval duty in the South Pacific, he had another family, and she had become a successful businesswoman. She raised her four children alone with the help of my grandparents. Living in rural Ohio, our family was always cautioned to be careful. To be silent. It was in school that I began to paint.

In our thirties, Sally became the financial officer for a big publishing company in New York City, and I became an artist who loved to teach. Every summer we would move to Provincetown where I lived in an old sea captain's house on Law Street and had a studio. Sally lived half a block away. I would always get there first with my kids, and when Sally arrived the first of every July with her kids, I baked her an apple pie.

We thought P-town was our town. She had two girls, and I had three boys. Sally would walk down Commercial Street and people would call out, "How are the boys?" And I would walk down Commercial Street and people would call out, "How are the girls?" We were lookalikes.

The Fourth of July parade in P-town is a joyous occasion year after year, and our children looked forward to it with great anticipation. The whole town turns out. There are fantastic costumes, impersonations, flags, dancing, and candies. And the blessing of the fleet for which all the Portuguese fishing boats are scrubbed, cleaned, and painted in the brilliant traditional orange. The fishermen, handsome and glorious, line up the boats in the bay and sail them one by one past the priest to be blessed. We would all celebrate! The incredible scope, spirit, the color, and the content of the creativity of the town stimulated and supported my work and life. I felt at home in this vibrant little town: the great expanse of sky and water, where everywhere and everyone was a visual treat. My creativity, my children, and my painting flourished.

Provincetown was the perfect playground. In the bay at the center of town my older kids dived for coins tossed to them by the tourists, and they fished off the dock. They caught so many fish that the fishermen often touched them for luck when they arrived in the early hours to start their day. There were abundant treasures all around us, including at the town dump, where we found five high-back chairs for our round table and painted them orange like the boats!

All this time we were drawing, painting, taking care of our kids, together. One day when we were thirty-three, and we were sitting on the beach watching the children swim, Sally turned to me and said, "Hazel, what would you like to do that you have never done before? . . . In your work, I mean." Well, I said, "In the schools they are teaching 'sex education' using godawful, sterile, unaesthetic illustrations. I would like to make a book like the Japanese Pillow Books in the Metropolitan Museum. They are beautiful books, illustrated with articulate and exquisitely drawn people and sexual images, intended to instruct young people in the art and passion of lovemaking!" "Why don't you?" Sally said. "Well," I said, "I can't draw without models because the images would be stereotypical and I want them to be seen and felt." "We'll pose for you," Sally said.

The next day, while the children were taking their naps, we put a mattress on the floor of my studio, and I drew Sally and Lennie (her husband). They were both tall, with very defined musculature, and beautiful. Standing at my drawing table and moving around them with a drawing pad, I drew fast with a sharp dark pencil. I quickly captured their overall forms, and I tried to study all their details: feet, hands, hair, and genitals. I paid close attention to how their bodies spoke to each other through touch. We had spent long summer days on the beach and in the ocean in our swimsuits. We were familiar, respectful. It was fun; it was funny. It was outrageous;

it was delicate. It required ultimate trust among all three of us and great sensitivity to know when it was time for me to leave the room.

Later, alone in my studio, I would hang all my studies on the wall around my drawing table, and, standing completely relaxed, I drew the final *Love Drawing,* paying close attention to the aesthetics to describe the softness and the feeling and passion between them. I always think of Sally and Lennie when I read a verse from Robert Creeley's poem "The Door": "Nothing for You is untoward. / Inside You would also be tall, / more tall, more beautiful. / Come toward me from the wall, I want to be with you." First published in his book *For Love,* these particular lines, I think, are about a muse, a source of inspiration. The drawings are about mutual acceptance, beauty, and connection. In my heart I have always felt a part of something larger, more expansive like the sky, or the ocean, or history. Even as a child I recognized this, and I fill that need through poetry, literature, and art. So words stimulate, support me. The Creeley poem sanctioned my need and desire to make this body of work.

After a drawing session we would celebrate. Sometimes with a good bottle of wine, or a sip or two of Fundador, or sometimes we would cook a good seven-course dinner. Maybe go dance in the back room at Cookie's Tap. Sometimes we would head back to the beach and skinny-dip in the ocean, lie on the dunes, and watch the stars.

Through the years there were sad times. Good times. Visits from our mothers. Times at the beach together. Bad times. Joyous times. Divine, loving times. Longnook Beach is known as one of the ten most beautiful beaches in the world. It is the first beach I saw on my initial trip to Provincetown. It was evening; the sun was low in the sky, and when I walked through the passage between the two huge sand dunes and THERE! THERE! was the ocean and the salt air, and the setting sun, I had a spiritual epiphany of being in a universe of color, light, sound, and joy where everything in the atmosphere was connected: past, present, and future. This experience inspired my work for the next sixty years.

The summer we were forty I said, "Sally, would you go to the Ace of Spades with me?" She said, "Why do you want to go there?" I said, "I am curious!" We put on our high heels and went together. It was the handwriting on the wall. The Ace of Spades was the only lesbian bar in Provincetown, and I just needed to be there.

In the winters I moved to the middle of the country. A place totally foreign to Sally. But her New York, her couch were also home. I came year after year, and sometimes three or four times. One year, I painted her a big painting for her new apartment in Independence Plaza, a ninety-inch triptych in her favorite colors. Reds, dark greens, and golds. Falling leaves. When we were two thousand miles apart, I loved picturing her sitting in her favorite ornately carved, high-back chair in front of her painting at her round table, and on one trip I did a life-size graphite drawing of her sitting in that chair. There was something familiar about that drawing, and I realized that because the image I drew was so deeply visual, so intimate, it captured her hidden underlying structure.

Sometimes I stayed in New York for a week, sometimes a month. Once when we were forty-six I rented a studio on Bleecker Street and stayed for several months. I would always cook and organize the kitchen. Sally loved it. She said, "Hazel, too bad I'm not attracted to women; you would suit me fine." We laughed. I kept a drawing book in a drawer under her couch. For years, hanging out, I drew people around her table. One Mother's Day dinner I did three drawings of Sally's mother and I saw the resemblance, but it was far too tenuous a thought to reveal this to Sally. As I returned from my sabbatical in New York to my Minneapolis college, and to my studio practice, I kept my thoughts to myself. But I never forgot.

Years later, Sally called. Her mother had died. She was devastated. I flew to New York to be with her. As I came in the door of her apartment, she said, "Hazel, sit down. I have something to tell you." I just looked at her and said, "She was your birth mother, wasn't she?" Sally asked, "How did you know?" And I said that years ago, as I was drawing her on Mother's Day, "I saw you hidden in her face."

Sad times. I lost a son. For five years he had leukemia. There were hospital trips, and emergency trips when he needed help, and celebrations when the treatments worked. Sally mothered my other boys. We said, "One mother is as good as another mother!" We still had Provincetown during our summers, and when the leukemia was in remission, we were all joyous. But then he died and Law Street was too sad for me. I moved out and Sally moved in. I still had her couch to call home in P-town. One summer when I was there, I painted a large painting for Law Street, for her. *Wolf Moon.* The full moon when everything aboveground is desolate and bereft, and everything underground is full of promise.

Bad times. Tough times! Several years later Sally lost her oldest daughter in a sudden, tragic death. We gathered on Staten Island to mourn her and to celebrate her life. The day was on the anniversary of my son's death. We grieved them both. I wrote: "After a child is born, a mother never sleeps." I stayed by my son's bed for twenty-one days and drew while he slept. It was automatic mark making from somewhere deep inside. *A Manifesto in 21 Days* is a record of his last days. Thirty-four drawings are now in the collection of the Weisman Art Museum. Art is healing, so I painted a Spirit Tree for Sally in memory of Lesley.

When Sally and I were fifty, I fell in love with Marcia. Together we went to New York to meet Sally, who was not surprised. We were drinking and talking and laughing, and when I left the room, Sally leaned over and said to Marcia, "You be good to her or I'll break your kneecaps!" Tough! They are both Leos! On the surface Leo is regal and independent, a powerful image. Beneath the surface Leos are very sensitive and perceptive. The prickly outer coating is their way of protecting their soft heart. I love these two Leos. Sally is always with me in my heart. Marcia is a philosopher and a painter. We share a studio, painting at opposite ends and stopping often to look at each other's work and have priceless dialogue. We have had many exhibitions together.

Marcia is very good for me. We were married in Provincetown in the old Congregational Church on Commercial Street. Sally gave us a party in the 8 Law Street yard. What a reception . . . singing and dancing and many, many, many friends. With Sally's blessing, and her special baked ham, we celebrated: wife and wife.

It was a challenge for Sally to travel from New York, but over the years, she came to the Heartland to visit me. One of those times was to be at the commencement when I was appointed an emeritus at a graduation ceremony. That time, in a quiet dinner, we toasted being sixty-two. One extremely cold winter in New York, she took a bus to Florida to join me and Marcia. We all sat on Vero Beach. Then in Provincetown for Sally's seventy-fifth birthday party, I made a lobster paella for seventy people to celebrate her. People just drifted into the yard from all over the country and gradually Sally recognized we were all there for HER.

The last time we were together was five beautiful days in May. We went to Chinatown for dinner. The next day we walked from Fifty-Third Street up Fifth Avenue to Ninety-Fourth Street. We stopped at the Guggenheim Museum to see the John Chamberlain Retrospective. We saw his sculpture, the *Belvo-Violet.* A found steel wall piece, it was still as powerful as it was in the 1960s when he made it, and it was emotionally moving to see its lasting strength. It reminded me of the line from Robert Creeley's poem about a muse: "Come toward me from the wall, I want to be with You."

In July Sally was seventy-nine. Her birthday was on a Tuesday. On Thursday we talked on the phone for over an hour. She in Provincetown and I in Grand Marais. She said she was fine. Slowing down. She died on Friday morning. Unique and unforgettable, she was my sister by choice. Marcia and I returned to Provincetown to celebrate her life where it ended at 8 Law Street. I have missed her for ten years.

For over fifty years Sally and I talked about art, politics, philosophy, people, death, love, and survival, and we laughed hard. I think of what she would say today. Our bodies are not our own. Personal choices and health care that we have planned on, worked for, and rejoiced in are eliminated. *Roe v. Wade* overturned. Women are still walking and praying for peace, and we are still working for equality. All we did, all we as artists, as women, as feminists, bound us together by our values and by our need for survival and beauty.

I find myself more and more urgent in my need to express the spirit of the *Love Drawings* that began in a conversation with Sally all those years ago on Law Street Beach. I want to champion the equality of all people. I want to continue speaking to serenity, strength, and beauty. Now, I am ninety. In my heart I will always stand nose to nose with Sally.

Dancing and Singing over the Years . . .

ADAR KAHIN

TRANSLATED BY FARDOUSA YOSSUF

Dancing weaves its way throughout Adar's life. She learned to dance at the age of three. She stops when asked about her early and middle years and says, "I don't want to talk about Somalia in those years. The Civil War."

Adar's story also reflects her timeless talent as a singer on her journey as a refugee: music across the decades.

When she came to the refugee camp in Kenya, she had a nine-day-old child. Even in the telling of the story, you can feel Adar's strength and, too, her sorrow.

In the camps were refugees who went in different directions, to other countries. She wonders why she came to such a cold place as Minnesota and pulls her coat closer as she sits in the back room of the Milkweed Coffee Shop.

"Always I needed school. I went to learn English, put my kids in day care, and worked at night." "She has strong energy, inner strength," says her friend, Fardousa Yossuf, who is a storyteller.

Suddenly Adar smiles and says, "I play jokes on Americans sometimes and say, with a straight face, 'Sometimes when our kids are too noisy, always interrupting our sleep, we have to kill them!'" She laughs then, at the way Americans look at her, not quite in disbelief, hurries to make clear she has told a joke.

She has made observations about raising children here . . . how in Somalia kids grow up with structure. You *tell* them to do things: "Close the door, go to bed, quiet down." Sometimes Americans *ask* their children, "Can you close the door? Would you please quiet down?" It is a subtle difference.

Adar's family and community are what matter to her. Her patience in teaching song and dance comes from a devotion to these experiences, not just for herself but for others. Music binds us, young and old.

In Somalia there is a respect for older adults. "We are given seats on the bus, helped across a street if we are frail."

Interweaving all parts of her life is dance, is song. Adar plans weekends at an organization called WellShare, an international organization that holds workshops and provides help for immigrants from all over the world. Women come and she leads them in dances. It is a time devoted to women, to stories, and to movement and the human voice.

Much of Adar's life is devoted to women, to keeping them engaged. At weddings she notes that women embrace together, share stories.

"Dancing is exercise!" she says, smiling.

Adar has organized and worked within the Somali community to provide "Tea and Talk" gatherings of women. The emphasis is on healthy living, dancing, being together. "Tea and Talk" is Adar's way of working and laughing and being in the presence of young and older women. It is a place to sing and to tell stories, to help each other.

Many of those she knows are fighting aging now. This calls Adar to hold even more gatherings where women can tell their stories, where their ideas are honored. Because women have so much responsibility, they often do not have enough time for themselves.

"If you don't show your feelings, depression can come to you. Sadness." Adar works to get help for all Somali women: to be engaged, to participate on their own in "Tea and Talk," acting, storytelling, and . . .

DANCING.

SINGING.

Adar Kahin is a force for good in so many ways in her community. What she brought from her home country is a fierce belief in women, in movement, and in joy. All the while she experiences some difficult days living in a country that does not always understand her ways.

Dancing is one way she brings all she knows to those she knows. Singing is another. Together they encompass hope.

For this essay Julie Landsman recorded the three-way conversation between herself, Adar Kahin, and Fardousa Yossuf, the translator. She put the text of the interview into essay form, received suggestions for revision from both translator and artist, and completed the final version.

Bringing It to the People

JAN ELFTMANN

During the time of Covid, ArtCar and ArtBike artists quickly figured out that in the name of social distancing, we could still bring our art form to the people! We drove out into the community. We were safe in our cars. We could park and stand outside, six feet apart, with our creative masks on and socialize!

So, every Saturday, for over sixty weeks, the ArtCar and ArtBike artists coordinated "Pop-Up Surprise Cruises" through our favorite neighborhoods. We drove by the homes of friends celebrating a birthday. We cruised by relatives living in senior homes. We surprised people working in their yards or out taking a walk. We saw little children peeking through the curtains of their home wondering about all the commotion of ArtCars honking their horns to announce our arrival.

I miss having that time in my life.

The artists bonded around bringing our art to the community. This was ArtCar and ArtBike Parading for the sake of art and connection. This was public art.

I miss the connections born of those crazy, scary times.

Houston, Texas, has the largest ArtCar Parade in the world. When my friend Dan moved there in 1995, he invited my husband and me to visit and experience their ArtCar Parade. It moved me.

I had never thought of using the car as the canvas! What a unique way to make a bold statement.

The direction of my art changed. I knew then and there, I wanted to create an ArtCar and be a part of something bigger than me.

But what to put on my ArtCar?

I was attracted to the cars that encrusted their vehicles with multiple objects. My husband reminded me of all the bags of corks I stored in our attic. Yes . . . so many corks!

So, the Cork Truck was born. A Mazda B2200 truck, covered with more than 10,000 wine and Champagne corks. I drove it every day and traveled in it everywhere, back and forth across the USA. People loved to talk with me and inquire about the Cork Truck.

The top two questions I got asked were:

1. Did you drink all that wine?
2. Does it float?

Answers:

1. It would take a bottle a day for twenty-eight years to drink that much wine! So, *no.*
2. It might, but I need to use it as my daily drive.

So, how did I get all those corks? I was a waitress at an Italian restaurant, putting myself through college. I was always looking for free art materials and fell in love with corks. I put out a wine bucket in the kitchen and asked coworkers to save the corks from the wine that they opened.

Gluing that first cork on my truck was a moment of freedom. I did not know anyone in Minnesota who glued objects onto their car. I had to research what glue to use: Liquid Nails, an outdoor tiling adhesive. I had to think about winter! How would cork survive our freezing-cold weather here? It turns out, cork is very resilient in all weather. I learned that cork does not absorb water; it compresses when water freezes around the cork and returns to its original shape when the water thaws. It does not burn. It does not decompose. Science!

Making my ArtCar was one part of being in this community of people who transform their modes of transportation into works of art. The other part was belonging.

In 1995, I organized a parade for a street fair for the artist organization Intermedia Arts. Our motto became "Every day is a parade for the ArtCar and ArtBike artists. We bring our art out of the studio and onto the streets to share with everyone!" Anyone was invited to join if they had a mode of transportation that was a work of art. No judgment. It was their vision. And there was no fee to join.

In 2024, we celebrated the thirtieth ArtCar and ArtBike Parade, which now cruises around Bde Unma (previously Lake Harriet) in Minneapolis. This is for the artists, hosted by the artists. It is small and intimate. Public Art.

Aging is a gift. I have history. I have experiences I carry with me. I have techniques.

And now that I have more time, I will make that new cork ArtCar and travel to explore new art environments and visit artists.

I want to create. I want to be in my studio and dream about the next piece of art.

And, I have time.

How Many Words Would I Need

TERESA ORTIZ

"I am an old woman now, how many words would I need to tell you about my life." This is a line I once wrote in a poem, and it explains both my reasons for writing and the challenge of writing at a mature age.

I grew up in Mexico City in the middle of the twentieth century. My family, who migrated to the capital from northern Mexico, had a long history of activism. They prided themselves on ancestors who homesteaded the deserts of southern Texas and northern Mexico and on grandparents who fought in the Mexican Revolution. I grew up listening to the history of my homeland. My mother loved to tell the stories of my family. My father liked to play with words, making up funny rhymes to entertain us as children. I was surrounded by words and tales and poetry. I was surrounded by the Mexican music that came from the radio: ranchero songs that depicted the lives of heroes, of women and men who tilled the soil or worked in the mines or fought in the Revolution, ballads that recounted tragic love stories, and tropical songs filled with rhythm and rhyme. My early writing as a youth was impregnated by these words, these verses, these tales: narratives from my Spanish/Arabic roots, from the inheritance of Sephardic rebels who populated the deserts of northern Mexico, who were my ancestors; by the songs filled with African rhythms, and by the sweet verses of our Mexica Indian forefathers.

I have seen so much in my lifetime, so many stories are crowded in my mind. I started writing as a very young person and I have written my entire life. I am a poet, a spoken word artist, and a fiction writer. I write in Spanish, my first language, and in English, the language I learned as an adult. My computer is filled with dozens of poems and short stories; some of them have been published, but many have not. I read my poems at events and perform spoken word poetry on a regular basis. But I am not a professional full-time writer. My daytime job, my profession, from which I recently retired, was as an educator. I taught children, youth, and adults to read and write in their own language and in a second language. Watching my students as they learned to read and write, as they learned a second language, was a tremendous feeling. Several of my adult students came from rural communities in Latin America, and they never had the opportunity to go to school. When I was in Chiapas, in southern Mexico, I worked with a group of Maya-speaking women who had never attended primary school. They were very excited about finally learning to read and write. And I felt the same accomplishment with my immigrant students in Minnesota. I loved my job, and I was very good at it.

My desire, upon retirement, was to turn my poetry and storytelling into a full-time career. Yet it has proved difficult to overcome transitions from schedules and routines, and stress, to mornings that open up with so many possibilities to create. Sometimes nothing comes out of my brain, and these possibilities open only into a blank white page with no words on it.

I have heard that many singers, as they age, lose their ability to sing; the cords in their throat get damaged and their voice no longer comes out. Many artists continue to produce until old age. Famous aging rockers like Mick Jagger or Keith Richards or Paul McCartney still perform. Old artists still paint, old writers still write—some of their best work comes with maturity and a lifetime of experience. But is this only the exception? Do most artists lose their vocal cords, their stamina to perform or paint, their ability to produce, or even lose their memories, their minds? How do mature artists deal with the reality of aging, with bodies and minds that deteriorate from wear and tear? As I face retirement from a job in education, I now encounter the possibility of a second career in literature. Can I still be a full-time professional writer at the age of seventy-five? This is when I ask myself: *Why* do I write? I write because I need to do it, because it is so important for me to tell the story. I write to keep memory alive.

When I was a child, I wanted to tell stories about girls like me. I was bored with fairy tales, which depicted girls patiently waiting for a knight or a prince to save them, to take them away. Instead, I wanted to tell the stories of women who took the world in their own hands, real women like my mother or my aunts, like my friends and my neighbors, like the women I knew and admired. One of these women was Tomasita, my mother's best friend, who, as a very young girl of sixteen, met and married her husband, a general in the revolutionary army of Francisco Villa. I loved to listen to her stories about the women who accompanied the fighters in battle, and the violence she witnessed in the civil war. As a widow in her fifties, and living only on a government pension, Tomasita raised her children to live successful lives: two of her daughters were prima ballerinas for the Folkloric Ballet, dancing in many of the world's capitals. Doris, my next-door neighbor and mother of my best friend, came to Mexico with her Jewish family, escaping World War II and the Holocaust. She was a writer for the local Jewish newspaper, writing in Spanish and Hebrew. Finally, there was my own mother, whose dream had been to study at a time when women were not allowed to go to college, yet she read every book available to her, knew more about history, politics, and international affairs than anything that I could have learned in school from my teachers.

As a young woman, I wrote what I was living. I wrote about my first experiences with the world outside my home. It was very early in my youth when I first encountered death and repression: in Mexico City in 1968. I wrote about growing up at a time when the world was changing in front of my eyes at the same time as I was growing from a girl to a woman. I wrote about the passion of struggle and the excitement of being involved in a social movement.

I was nineteen years old in 1968, a freshman at the University of Mexico. In September of that year, the Mexican Student Movement started after a group of students from a downtown high school were brutally attacked by the police, and all schools and universities went on strike to stop police brutality. My classmates and I participated in the movement, talking with students and their families, passing information and flyers throughout the city, participating in marches and rallies and feeling the excitement of a movement that, we believed, would bring democracy and justice to Mexico. We were harassed and attacked by the police, and many of our classmates were taken to jail. On October 2, when we were at a rally with thousands of other students at a large plaza in the Tlatelolco neighborhood of Mexico City, the Mexican army and police attacked the meeting, shooting at the crowd from high buildings and surrounding the plaza with tanks. People started running in all directions to save their lives. My friend and I found shelter in a basement apartment as the owners opened their door to anybody trying to escape the shooting. About a hundred people hid there, with the lights off, for many hours. We were able to get out around midnight, after the massacre was over. Hundreds of students were taken to jail or were injured, and three hundred people were killed. My best male friend spent two weeks in jail and one of our classmates was among those who died. This event changed my life forever. I was never the same person after that.

As a member of the 1970s generation, I lived at a time of tremendous excitement, and when I moved to the United States, I not only lived the life of a new immigrant, but I also experienced the amazing youth movement that was happening in this country at that time. This life of activism was only a continuation of what I lived in Mexico. From the '70s to the '80s, I lived the history of my homeland (Mexico) and of my adopted land (United States): student movements, civil rights, antiwar organizing, feminism, and the plight of immigrants in the United States.

In the 1990s, while living and working in Central America and southern Mexico, I learned about and experienced from the people around me the inheritance of five hundred years of colonialism in the Americas. I understood the struggle for antiracism, Indigenous rights, and the Zapatista movement with the promise of a better life for all. All the time I was writing poems and stories to capture what I was seeing, hearing all around me. In the first years of the twenty-first century, I worked with Latino immigrants in the Twin Cities on their labor rights and taught them English while helping them to incorporate into this society.

During all these years, I listened to people, I was a witness to history, and I lived it. My poems and short stories were impregnated with these experiences.

Today, at the age of seventy-five, I continue to write because I have a need to tell the stories that have not completely been told before, as well as stories that have been forgotten. These are the stories that were not always learned by new generations. These are the stories that were erased from our history textbooks.

Today, as I listen to young women talk about feminism and how patriarchy is their inheritance from the older generations, I remember when, in the 1970s, my women friends and I had to defend ourselves in the streets of Mexico City against men who harassed us. I can picture even now how we fought with whatever we had at hand (purses, grocery bags, hairbrushes) to defend ourselves. I remember, too, when I was sexually assaulted in downtown Minneapolis and had to run away as fast as I could to save my life. I remember abortions under dangerous circumstances. Even now I can remember how we had to struggle for liberation and change. Today I understand more than ever how women's liberation persists; the realization that we need to continue fighting with everything at hand, and we have the obligation to write about it.

Today, as we face the threat of authoritarianism, I am reminded of the people I met and with whom I shared my life in Guatemala and El Salvador in the 1990s. They had survived decades of repression and genocide yet were still struggling for freedom and continuing to fight with all their strength and determination to find peace and justice in their countries, in their homes, and in their lives. Now in 2025 USA I can picture so clearly the refugees from Chile and Argentina, whom I met and interviewed in Mexico and the United States. I remember their courage in their fight, and their unwavering hope of the possibility of restoring democracy and justice in their homelands. I think about my neighbors and my friends in the States who came from all over Latin America and many other places of the world, who walked for miles to get here. I was in touch with those escaping violence and threats to their lives. Once here these immigrants live productive, hardworking lives, raising their children with dreams in their souls. One of them was Dulce, a young single mother from Mexico, who came to Minnesota with her two young sons, supporting them here by making and selling tamales as she learned English and survived in a foreign environment. Today her sons have finished college, and she runs a radio program at a local station, informing the immigrant Latino community about their rights. My student Wilin and his siblings came from Guatemala as teenagers, traveling alone and with nothing, and here, after several years and through hard work, today they manage a successful family-owned hamburger joint. I think of these stories and many others when I feel down, when I cannot write.

I think of my own ancestors, of my grandparents, and I remember my mother's words: "Don't be afraid: you come from a family of revolutionaries." I think of my own life, a survivor of repression and massacres. I think of the people I have loved who passed away before me, my parents, my two brothers, and especially I think of my son, an activist who lived his life with the belief that this world can be changed to make it better. I think of what I learned from all of them, how courageously they lived their lives. And when I lose all hope as so much is happening around me politically and socially—and even in my personal life—I am called to remember the Indigenous people of southern Mexico, the Zapatistas of Chiapas, fighting to build a world of equality: a movement that surpassed borders and that gave faith to youth all over the planet. I remember all that and so I feel obligated to write, to share their hope and mine through my words.

As I face retirement and old age, writing becomes very hard. Some days I would rather read or do other things. Writing is just too hard. It seems that my mind is as blank as the page on which I write.

When that happens, I relax, I breathe, and I remind myself: I write to honor those who came before me. Writing is my obsession and my need, even when it is hard. I have accumulated so many experiences throughout my life, I have seen so much, that I feel I have an obligation to share it.

So, now, today, I am very excited that I am able to write more poems, more short stories, more narratives. I am excited to be a poet and a storyteller. I am excited and honored to be able to tell the stories of my ancestors and my loved ones, and my neighbors and my land.

I am excited to keep the memories from dying.

Two Poems and a Memory

JULIA DINSMORE

American Koolaid

america's koolaid was spiked long ago.

like back when the founding fathers
wanted to bestow life & liberty to
white land-owning men only.

back when the spiritual dissonance
of slave owning religion
and "killing the Indian to save the man"
branded Black folk 3/5ths human
and Indigenous peoples savage.

america's koolaid features
time-release efficacy.

imbedded itself into the DNA
of our collective imagination
to the degree that
social scientists say
a large %

of american whites
are trapped in a coma:
tethered to structural life-support systems
that keep us immobile.

some hell of a koolaid
brewed in the hearth of lies.

i prefer truth to any kind of drug
that numbs a conscience
or stunts the maturation of a soul.

Thinking now about my ancestors
I believe they must have
Given me some antibodies to lies

'cause in my blood
there is american koolaid *resistance*

though from the perspective of
being an elder
I gotta admit,
some days
that coma state looks attractive.

but only for moments.

Then the friction gets
white hot
for not living fully in the truth,
for spending even a moment
under the influence
of american koolaid's temptation.

Hopscotch

the subduction zone
of tectonic shifts on repeat
and
the real stuff
of
my
burning mantle
cut
fault lines
where ruptured earth
rearranges
personal continents and oceans.
frequently
shape-shifting ground
liquifies
many a way forward
oh shit.
pressures
quake and shear
craggy geospiritual territories
into new ideas
on
how to be in this world
and
be
not
of
it.
Furthermore
i will learn magic

to keep tsunami
from extinguishing
this here
fire.

Neighbor Women

Two women stand out in the memory of where I and my children lived the longest in South Minneapolis. We moved five times into different dwellings on that same block. We'd arrived to our version of suburbia, which was a few streets south of Lake Street, and we worked hard to stay there, while two neighbors toiled to leave. Both women were trapped in dangerous marriages and they each devised protracted, courageous escape plans.

One mama of two began mailing forks, knives, articles of clothing and other household items to her people down south in one of the Carolinas. She sent packages piece by piece, month after month, and after a few years she made her break. She told me how mailing bits of her life was the pivotal part of her action plan that enabled a bearable existence until timing was right to flee.

The other woman had five children and needed to go back home to London. Every Friday for over two years she operated a porch sale. Her wares were scavenged from garbage picking, the free store, bag sales at churches, the last hours of garage sales. She eventually squirreled away enough money for the flight overseas. To safety.

Some of the neatly coifed, polite society neighbors clucked away in judgment regarding "those people's" unruly lives for not expressing appropriate shame regarding their circumstances. I wondered if people thought they were perhaps too public about their needs? These attitudes were confusing to my way of interpreting these situations: I saw creative survival, ingenious love, and self-preservation on fleek.

Observing people find ways out of no way, enduring much, persevering. As I age, I see more and more women and men triumphing over poverty, danger, the lack of resources. They have always taught me valuable knowledge, knowledge I have needed to survive myself. Observing indifference by people who are scornful has shown me how I do not want to be.

I feel deep gratitude for being able to help and witness my two neighbor women's strength and grit. To think about them again, years later, has encouraged me to keep writing, keep teaching, keep raising my grandchildren in homes where they will see a real version of bravery and creativeness.

The mirror and other things I purchased at the porch sales are still with me, after eight more moves. Precious belongings. Precious memories.

Living Well

MARCIE R. RENDON

At ninety-seven, Gloria Miguel, Spiderwoman Theater, is in town after performing *Misdemeanor Dream* with Spiderwoman collective. Spiderwoman, envisioned by Muriel Miguel with her two sisters, Gloria and Lisa, was formed in 1976 out of the feminist era of that time. They use story weaving to create and express ideas from a Native woman's lens. Spiderwoman is the longest running Native theater company in the United States.

In February 2024, they toured to Vermillion, South Dakota, for a week of performance and workshop, then took a bus to Duluth to perform at two venues before moving on to the Fond du Lac Tribal college, where they performed *Misdemeanor Dream* and conducted acting workshops before coming to the Twin Cities to once again perform and conduct workshops.

We have dinner at a local Greek restaurant. Gloria is beautiful. Pure white hair frames her perpetually tan face. Her eyes engage you as she talks about performing and how this stint has left her tired, but she is recovering just fine. She tells me she is currently writing a piece about aging and that we'll have our annual dinner when she returns next year.

Last year she came to dinner with a walker. This year a wheelchair. She wonders if on her next tour someone might need to carry her. She has no plans for quitting.

Ninety-seven. Mind intact. Still performing. Next week she will do a podcast for the American Indian Family Center in St. Paul. Still being generous with her knowledge and talent.

My first theater workshop was in the early '90s at the Playwright Center and was conducted by Spiderwoman. I remember that for most of the afternoon I was a tree blowing in the wind. I had no idea what I was doing or the journey I was embarking on. I did not grow up with access to theater or with any idea that someday I myself would write plays. I had arrived at the workshop because they were the "Indian thing" happening that day and my mind and heart was hungry for role models and possibilities. Thirty-some years later, at seventy-two, I am older than Gloria was that day, and she is still inspiring me to live each day.

What is she role modeling for me?

Gloria embodies self-care. Her hair is styled. Turquoise-and-silver rings circle fingers on both hands. Dressed impeccably. She tells me she visited her doctor before traveling and they told her she is in fine health. Just to be sure, she will visit them again when she gets home to New York City. Self-care. Self-esteem. Self-worth.

Gloria continues to use her mind. She is always creating. Forever the performer. Forever perfecting her craft. She belongs to a writing group beyond Spiderwoman, other writers, other creatives. We have conversation about world affairs and the implications for Indigenous people around the world. She asks about my children and tells me about her daughter who lives closer to her.

After a short conversation about pretendians and how sad the whole situation with Buffy Sainte-Marie is, we have a long, heated conversation with her son and his partner about tribal enrollment, discrimination within tribes against mixed-heritage people, and whether or not it is worth the effort to be enrolled. We talk about the political, historical, and generational implications attached to tribal enrollment. The conversation drifts to how much she loves New York and will probably never live anywhere else.

I am in awe of her creative talent, her sharp, engaging mind, and what must be her determination in the face of physical aging. Gloria is not in denial about aging. She is certain about living. Whether from willpower or decision she has decided to continue living fully each day.

I want to be just like Gloria Miguel when I grow up.

Mi'iw.

Contributors

SHARI ALBERS is an artist, writer, community activist, and Minneapolis history nerd. As a junior high art teacher in her twenties, Albers specialized in drawing and ceramics. In her thirties, she designed presentations and built sets for a multimedia company before starting a family and freelancing her artistry. She created logos and theme graphics, designed books and brochures, and illustrated children's stories. She was focusing on writing and illustrating picture books for children when her husband's death launched another path. Her "Widow Series" has been exhibited at Twin Cities and Wisconsin art centers.

HEND AL-MANSOUR's work highlights the power of women through figurative representations in an Islamic art style. She often centers stylized figures against a background of Arabic calligraphy, Islamic geometric design, and traditional Saudi women's art. She uses installation, screen printing, and murals, often combined, and her artistic repertoire has expanded to include 2D animation. She holds a Master of Fine Arts and a Master of Art History from the Minneapolis College of Art and Design and the University of St. Thomas, respectively, and has received grants from the Minnesota State Arts Board and the Metropolitan Regional Arts Council, the McKnight Fellowship, and the Jerome Fellowship.

HAZEL BELVO is a painter and a teacher often called *A Matriarch of Art,* which is the title of her biography by Julie L'Enfant. An exhibiting artist since 1960, she is an emerita professor at the Minneapolis College of Art and Design; a founding member of WARM, a feminist art gallery; and a Bunting Fellow at Radcliffe Harvard University. Born in Ohio, she lived in New York City in her studio on the Lower

East Side. She was recently celebrated with a sixty-year retrospective at the Minnesota Museum of American Art, *For Love,* curated by Laura Joseph.

CHRIS CINQUE is a visual artist living and working in Minneapolis. Her work touches a primal place that has an invigorating visceral component, creating interactions between the viewer and the viewed, including what both bring to the experience emotionally, psychically, and spiritually, opening doors from this concrete moment to that unexpected correlation. Chris taught ELL to adults for twenty years and was a theater artist for more than twenty years before that. She is a member of Form+Content Gallery.

VENUS DE MARS is best known as the transgender leader of the glam-punk band Venus de Mars & All the Pretty Horses. Venus came out as trans in 1988, making her one of the first openly trans artists in the industry, at a time when identifying as trans meant being classified as having a mental perversion and living as an outcast. Her refusal to live a shadow existence, instead embracing her uniqueness, complicated her musical and artistic career paths. She is writing a memoir reflecting on her thirty-seven-year trans journey.

JULIA DINSMORE is a mother and grandmother living in the Twin Cities of Minnesota and deeply committed to her communities there. She is an author, poet, singer-songwriter, and poverty abolitionist, best known for her poem “My Name Is Not Those People.” She uses creative voice and storytelling to talk about the one thing we too often ignore: class and poverty in America. Though functionally illiterate for most of her life, Julia taught herself how to write while writing her first book, *My Name Is Child of God, Not Those People: A First Person Look at Poverty.*

MARY MOORE EASTER, a dancer and choreographer, is the founder of the dance program at Carleton College. Her books include her memoir *The Way She Wants to Get There: Telling on Myself* (a Minnesota Book Award finalist), the anthology *What Wakes Her in the Night,* and the poetry collections *From the Flutes of Our Bones*; *The Body of the World* (a Minnesota Book Award finalist); *Walking from Origins*; and *Free Papers: Poems Inspired by the Testimony of Eliza Winston, a Mississippi Slave Escaped to Freedom in Minnesota in 1860.* She has been a Cave Canem Fellow and has received numerous performance awards and grant support.

JAN ELFTMANN's goal as an artist is to create art that encourages an audience to pause, wonder, and, perhaps, interact with her work. She incorporates art into her everyday life in hopes of encouraging conversations between people and transcending the boundaries that separate us. She has a strong commitment to and involvement in the local art community. She is an ArtCar artist and the director of the ArtCar ArtBike Parade; an artist with the Art Shanty Projects on frozen lakes in the winter; the curator of 801 Gallery in the Minneapolis North Loop neighborhood; and a teaching artist.

GEORGIA A. GREELEY lives and works in St. Paul. She is a writer and visual artist, interdisciplinary in thought and deed. Historically, her work has been seen in fine press broadsides, handmade artist's books, and limited-edition fine press books. Her creative practice is in transition: she is adding calligraphy and stitching to earlier mediums. Her writing focuses on poetry and children's literature, but she often works in many other genres.

KATHRYN HADDAD has received fellowships and awards from the Bush Foundation, the Playwrights' Center, Jerome Foundation, Minnesota State Arts Board, AARP, and McKnight Foundation. She received the 2018 Kay Sexton Award from the Friends of the Saint Paul Public Library. Her plays and nonfiction have been performed and published throughout the United States on stage and in anthologies. She cofounded and directed Pangea World Theater and Mizna Arab Arts Organization, and is now the founding executive artistic director of New Arab American Theater Works. She taught language arts in the public schools for thirty-four years and continues to work as a writer and culture bearer in the local and national Arab American community.

KIM HINES is a multifaceted artist whose career spans fifty-eight years. She is a second-generation Minnesotan, and her art encompasses playwriting, directing, acting (retired), education, and visual art. Her plays have been staged across the United States and internationally. Five of her plays were commissioned by the Kennedy Center, and her play *Home on the Morning Train* is a staple in children's theater curricula. She has ventured into music, writing the libretto for *Sincerely Yours, Pauli Murray.* Her YA novella *Wingo-Fly* captivates readers of all ages. Returning to visual art, Hines creates unique collage vignettes for her greeting card collection.

CAROLYN HOLBROOK was named the McKnight Distinguished Artist in 2025. She is founder and director of More Than a Single Story. Her memoir, *Tell Me Your Names and I Will Testify,* won a Minnesota Book Award in 2021. She is coeditor of the anthology *We Are Meant to Rise: Voices for Justice from Minneapolis to the World* and coauthor of Josie Johnson's memoir, *Hope in the Struggle.* Her 2022 TEDx talk was presented at Concordia College, and her awards include the Kay Sexton Award; Hamline University Exemplary Teacher; 50 over 50; Celebrate the Sistahs; and Flowers Now!

ADAR KAHIN plans weekends at WellShare, an international organization that provides workshops and help for immigrants from all over the world. She supports women and their needs and enhances their chance to connect with each other during these events devoted to women, stories, and movement.

DEBORAH KEENAN is the author of eleven poetry collections, including *The Saint of Everything* and *Willow Room, Green Door: New and Selected Poems,* which received the Minnesota Book Award. She is also author of *from tiger to prayer,* a book of writing ideas. A professor in the MFA Program at Hamline University for thirty years, she continues to teach at the Loft Literary Center. Mom of four, grandmother of four, she lives by the confluence of the Minnesota and Mississippi rivers in beautiful, mysterious St. Paul.

AMOKE KUBAT founded Yo Mama's House Cooperative in North Minneapolis. Yo Mama's philosophy and practice is to empower mothers by disrupting the devaluation of women's visible and invisible labor and increasing the social and political recognition of the Art of Mothering through Art Making.

JULIE LANDSMAN is a writer of nonfiction and poetry. She discovered painting at the age of sixty-two and enjoys both watercolor and oil. Her books include *Basic Needs: A Year with Street Kids in a City School, A White Teacher Talks about Race,* and *Growing Up White.* Her essay "Words, Images, and Music: How We Enter" won the Bechtel Award from Teachers and Writers Collaborative, and she has edited five anthologies about race and education. Her short stories and poems have been published in many magazines.

FIONA MCCRAE worked as an editor at the publisher Faber and Faber, first in London and then in Boston. In 1994, she moved to Minnesota to become the publisher and director of the innovative and award-winning literary publisher Graywolf Press, and she retired in 2022. She is vice-chair of the National Book Foundation and serves on the board of *Orion* magazine. She is working on a series of essays about memory loss, which runs in her family. She lives in Minneapolis with her husband, John Coy, who writes books for young people.

TERESA ORTIZ, a spoken word poet and fiction writer, is an immigrant from Mexico living in Minnesota. She is a published author of short stories, poetry, and nonfiction and has performed throughout Minnesota as a member of the Latino collective Palabristas. She writes in English and Spanish to honor her loved ones, aiming to portray her identity, the land where she has lived, and the lives that have touched her.

REBECCA PAVLENKO, photographer and visual artist, has received Minnesota State Arts Board and Metropolitan Regional Arts Council grants. She taught workshops and classes and was a mentor in the

WARM Mentors/Protégés program. She was a founding member of Women in Photography and Visual Arts and a scenic artist on more than one hundred productions at the Guthrie Theater. Her photography grows out of her love of nature, Zen practice, and joy in exploring photographic materials. She is fascinated by the psychology of the human spirit, the interconnection of all things, and the symbolic lessons that are nature's gift.

MARCIE R. RENDON, citizen of the White Earth Nation, is the bestselling author of *Where They Last Saw Her* and the Cash Blackbear crime series. Her poetry collection, *Anishinaabe Songs for the New Millennium,* was published by the University of Minnesota Press, and she is also author of *Stitches of Tradition,* a picture book. Mni Giizhik Theater is producing her scripts *Say Their Names* and *Sweet Revenge.* She was the 2020 McKnight Artist of the Year; named a 50 over 50 Change-maker by Minnesota AARP and POLLEN; and listed in Oprah's 2020 list of thirty-one Native American authors to read. But mostly, she's known as Grandma.

DEBRA J STONE is a 2023–25 Jerome Hill Arts Fellow in Literature. Her debut novel, *The House on Rondo,* about the destruction of the St. Paul Black community of Rondo Avenue in 1963, was published by the University of Minnesota Press. Her writing has been published by *Blue Earth Review, Indiana Review, Green Mountains Review, Under the Gum Tree,* and other literary journals, and her poem "year-of-staying-in place" was Best of Net and nominated for the Pushcart Prize. She is a board member of the Hennepin History Museum. www.debrajeannestone.com.

JOYCE SUTPHEN was Minnesota's Poet Laureate from 2011 to 2021. Her first book, *Straight Out of View,* won the Barnard New Women Poets Prize; *Coming Back to the Body* was a finalist for a Minnesota Book Award; and *Naming the Stars* received a Minnesota Book Award in poetry. She is professor emerita at Gustavus Adolphus College in St. Peter, Minnesota.

SUZANNE THAO was born Xyo Mim (in reference to the first star next to the moon) Vaj in Phou Mou, Long Cheng, Laos. She learned Hmong paj ntaub (Hmong embroidery) from her paternal grandmother, Mee Xiong, and her mother, Chia Lo. Since 2016, she has partnered with the Hmong Museum to teach Project Paj Ntaub, a monthly class on two traditional Hmong paj ntaub techniques, cross-stitch and appliqué. She offers mentoring to those who need support for difficult stitches or projects.

JOANN VERBURG is a visual artist who has also supported other artists' projects since her first job at the Philadelphia Museum of Art. She grew up in the rolling hills of New Jersey, surrounded by Italian Americans, and has written observations in a diary or journal since childhood that, in many ways, are the equivalent of snapshots. She has innovated with form to invite viewers into a present-moment experience that has been called "resplendent" (Max Lakin, *New York Times,* 2022) and that "linger[s] in a mood of deliberate stillness, where measured contemplation and quiet reflection actually have room to blossom" (Loring Knoblauch, collectordaily.com). Her photo/video exhibitions include *Present Tense: JoAnn Verburg* at MoMA (New York); *JoAnn Verburg: AFTERSHOCKS* at the Minneapolis Institute of Art; and *The Migration of Birds* at Palazzo Mauri (Spoleto, Italy).

MORGAN GRAYCE WILLOW's poetry collections and chapbooks include *Dodge & Scramble, Between, Silk, Oddly Enough,* and *The Maps Are Words.* Her writing has been published in anthologies and journals such as *Broad Wings, Long Legs*; *Queer Nature*; *Ecopoetics*; *North American Review*; and *Third Coast.* Her prose publications include the title memoir in *Riding Shotgun* and the essay "(Un) Document(ing)" in *Water~Stone Review.* Her visual work includes the artist book *Collage for Mina Loy* as well as collages in *Saint Paul Almanac* and online in *Concision Poetry Magazine.* She is a teaching artist with the Loft Literary Center and the COMPAS Artful Aging program.

DIANE WILSON is a Dakota author, educator, and bog steward who has published five award-winning books as well as numerous essays. Her novel *The Seed Keeper* and her memoir *Spirit Car: Journey to a Dakota Past* won Minnesota Book Awards. She has written a nonfiction book, *Beloved Child,* and a middle-grade biography, *Ella Cara Deloria*, and coauthored the picture book *Where We Come From*. She is enrolled on the Rosebud Reservation and a Mdewakanton descendant. She lives on ten acres north of the Twin Cities and cares for a Tamarack bog.

MIEKO YAMAZAKI was born in Japan and graduated from university in Tokyo, majoring in music. After teaching music for a year at a middle school, she became a Japanese language teacher for Japanese as Second Language students in Japan and the United States for fifteen years. When she came to Minnesota, the spacious Minnesota landscape inspired her to paint. Since graduating from Minneapolis College of Art and Design in 2001, she has been painting abstractions in oils, utilizing chemical reactions with paints and medium.